Since We Woke Up

LESSONS FROM TWO YEARS OF LIVING ON A SCHOOL BUS

BY
TAWNY MCVAY

WITH A FOREWORD BY
MICHAEL MCVAY

White Bus Press

ISBN: 978-0-578-97428-6 (Paperback)
LCCN: 2021916016

Printed in the United States of America.

Since We Woke Up
www.sincewewokeup.com
info@sincewewokeup.com

First paperback edition October 2021
10 9 8 7 6 5 4 3 2 1

FOR MY CONSTANTS IN A WORLD OF CHANGE.

To Mike, you are my only home, and the sun my world revolves around.

To Evan, still my rock after all this time.

To Aidyn, my biggest fan.

And to Ely, who keeps me humble and gives the best hugs.

AND TO OLIVER.

Our home and adventure. This one's for you buddy.

Table of Contents

Since We Woke Up

Foreword

When Tawny and I met in 2011, I was fresh out of the military. My life experience, at that point, consisted of high school, boot camp, military shenanigans, and a failed marriage. Looking back on that day, I think I knew I had just met my future wife, although we spent several months in denial, dancing around the inevitable. We grew to be close friends, sharing and embracing every aspect of each other's life. This, of course, included her long-kept desire to be a writer. That was more than ten years ago.

During our time together, Tawny never abandoned the idea of one day writing a book and becoming an author. Unfortunately, life has its way of delaying our goals and interrupting our plans, we all know this. Between my time spent back in the military, both of us pursuing careers in the nursing field, opening a gym, and starting a nomadic life, it seemed like she never had the time or space to bury herself in writing. As frustrating as I am sure it was for her, I believe it was destined to be this way.

To my knowledge, Tawny's life has never been uneventful, but I think she was subconsciously waiting for the right moment to author her first book. She certainly didn't wait this long because she lacked the talent. Friends and family members have always exclaimed over Tawny's proclivity for writing, which can only be described as deeply elegant and richly poetic. She's spent years building hundreds of thousands of followers on social media, simply through her genuine creativity and unique ability to captivate audiences with her gift for storytelling. In truth, it will never cease to amaze me how she can take a seemingly simple experience or thought and turn it into something profound and beautiful.

So ten years after our relationship began, when Tawny told me she was going to write a book, my immediate thought was, "It's about damn time." It was in this latest chapter of our life together that the stars aligned in such a way that writing a book became almost inexorable for her. Tawny had created the life she'd always wanted. She had the space, the freedom, the inspiration, and, of course, an amazing husband who throws his full weight into supporting her dreams.

Since We Woke Up is a compelling memoir of Tawny's journey to find her own version of happiness. However, this is no generic tale of true love, hardships, motherhood, or failed marriages. Sure, you will find these stories included in her book, as they are fundamental aspects of her story, but Since We Woke Up is about so much more than these singular events. This book is about teaching people how to identify and pursue their own happiness, whatever it looks like. It's about showing people that by being brave, and daring to turn away from expectations, they can truly find freedom, and thus, the happiness they've always searched for.

Obviously, as Tawny's husband, I am, and forever will be, her biggest fan. Biased as I might be, my words can hardly express the depth of this book nor the value of the messages within its pages. There are many couples like us. There are other nomads traveling around in converted school buses. Knowing many of these people personally, I can say they are all beautifully unique souls. But I assure you, there is only one Tawny, and this is her story.

Michael McVay

Acknowledgements

The number of people I need to thank for their part in this story is vast and could ramble on for innumerable pages if allowed, but I will try to keep it brief.

My little nontraditional family are the reason this book had space to be written, and the people who have held me through the lowest points of my life so I could write it during a high one. Obviously at the top of the list is Mike. The story within these pages would be so very different without you. For a decade you've been my friend, lover, adventure buddy, shoulder to cry on, workout partner, and constant reminder that every day is a new one to dream. From the notes you leave all over the bus for me to the way you shake me out of my work to make sure I eat, know it's your love that both sustains and inspires me. Evan, no words can do justice to exactly how unselfish and encompassing your love is or how terrible your dad jokes are. I'm grateful for both. Aidyn and Ely, you are without a doubt the best work of my life, and most of the meaning I've found within it.

Our families are right under that for years of support and love and inspiration. Especially my in-laws, Ron and Linda, for opening up your home to us when we were at our lowest and giving us a place, physically and emotionally, to weather the storm, my mom, Rhonda, for the constant support and encouragement when I needed it most, and my dad, James, and brothers Levi, Brendon, and Jeremiah, without whom Oliver wouldn't exist as he does now. Brendon and Jeremiah put in hours of manual labor helping us with random projects, and it's Levi's genius that helped me finally understand the nuances of solar systems. My dad contributed so many hours to this bus and my vision for it that I will never be able to properly thank him. From the custom metal door he made with the original bus windows to the wood stove and refrigerator surrounds, helping us run plumbing and propane systems, and infinite projects in the last two years, his years of knowledge and willingness to drop everything to help his daughter is above and beyond, even for a dad. More so since he came into my life so late and didn't really have to choose to be one, especially to someone who made his life hell for the first few years he was in hers. From the gym to this bus to every random whim I come up with, you've supported me more than I had a right to expect and far more than I deserve, and I love you so much.

The members of our gym, especially the ones who were there from the beginning and stuck with us to the bitter end. You made life bearable at the point it was lowest for us, supporting our dreams even when it meant losing something meaningful to yours. There are so many of you to whom this shoutout belongs, but especially to the core group that still texts and calls and lets us know we aren't forgotten even though the gym has been closed for years, you are the reason we did what we did for so long. One of the greatest honors of my life will always be having been your Satawny. Stef, Michelle, Brandy, Jamie, and Jessica – you're at the very top of that list for the coffee dates and long talks and helping me believe in myself with your encouragement and endless rounds of laughter.

To the women in my life who have meant so much to it and given me examples of who I wanted to be. Charley, you will forever be my bestest. Bonnie, you were the first to make me feel like it was okay to be fully myself. Joniene, I spent most of my life trying to follow in your footsteps and be just like you. Stef, Michelle, and Brandy, you've collectively held more space for me than anyone else ever has. Trish, you held this vision of my life for me on days I couldn't see it. Brooke, your endless love has gotten me through some rough days. Lauren, you're my spot of sun in dark moments, a constant encouragement. Torie, you're my best mate, mate, and I can't wait to adventure with you. And Sue, my Sue. My greatest wish is to be just like you when I grow up.

To every single person who follows our journey across our social media platforms and gave me a place to tell our story while you cheered, supported, and generally loved us from afar — thank you. This story would have unfolded regardless of whether or not we told it out loud, but sharing it with you and having you along for the ride took it to a whole other level of fun. You say we inspired you, but on low days, it was you who got us through and gave us the inspiration we needed to keep going. Every comment, every DM, every email, the people who stop on the road to talk to us and tell us they follow us, those who share our content and promote it — thank you.

To the crew at I-State who helped us find our bus and make sure it was the right one, and to John and Hilaree especially, for the mechanical support and constant love, thank you friends.

And finally, to the nomadic community. You guys were our inspiration and support network while we built and got started in this life, and now, we're privileged to called so many of you our friends. Every single one of you we've met, both online and in person, inspire us in some way. The people in this little niche of the world are among the bravest, most creative, big-hearted, supportive, and loving we've ever met, and we are honored to be part of it. Sharing campfires and endless cups of coffee and laughs crowded in one of our tiny homes has been the single best part of this life, and I hope to meet every one of you I haven't already someday out on the road we all call home.

Preface

Writing this book was one of the hardest things I've ever done. Not because I didn't want to, not because the story wasn't waiting to be told, and certainly not because I was at a loss for words about the experiences we've had living in this old school bus.

This book is an extension of the social media pages bearing the same name, and it's in those little squares pieces of this tale first unfolded. As I worked back through our story, it was those posts with their limited characters I found myself scrolling through to remember specific moments, and they became the inspiration for the chapters you're about to read and the words they contain. I didn't need to build an outline of the tale I was about to tell, because it was already there on our feed, written alongside photos and videos as we lived it.

And therein was my problem. We've lived so much of our life in the open over these last few years, finding a way to tell the same story we'd already shared so much of was intimidating. Like extracting fossilized bones from the ground in order to clean them off and assemble them together again into a complete skeleton for viewing, I found myself paralyzed at the start, petrified once I'd unearthed these old stories, I would never be able to put them back together again in a way that made sense. I dallied. I wrote the first chapter and deleted it more times than I can count. Second guessed my starting point repeatedly, moving it around and around. Maybe I should start at the very beginning and tell an ordered tale. Maybe I should start at the end and look back through time toward where it all started.

Then the whole project sat dormant for a while as I agonized over it, deciding perhaps I didn't have a worthwhile tale to tell. Just because some people followed us on social media and thought our story was cool didn't immediately translate to a book, after all. But it was there, growing inside me, screaming to come out. I'd find myself jotting notes in my journal on a page titled "Book". Waking up in the middle of the night with an idea. Thinking about how this random thought or that could be the glue that held a particular set of bones together.

And slowly, between the pages of that journal and talks with Mike and bookmarked social media posts, the story of how we came to live on a bus and what we learned in the process took shape. It isn't really that profound a story, to be honest. Just one about two people who decided to live on a bus, the same way thousands of others have lived in vehicles for decades. But it is a relatable one, I think. Maybe even an inspiring one. It's the love story I didn't mean to write, about a life I didn't plan for, where I met a version of myself I didn't know existed.

I will apologize in advance for how often our social media comes up in these pages, but as these platforms are now a large part of our world, my job, and the trailer, so to speak, of this book, it naturally pops up as part of our tale. And because it was the start of this story, and my inspiration to tell this expanded one, I actually began each chapter with the post it was inspired by.

Writing this book gave me a completely new round of gratitude for my life, as I stepped back through time into the photos and captions to relive those moments. When we decided to live on a school bus, I was only looking for a way out of a life I felt trapped in. I was willing to trade in my large home and most of our possessions for this little one, hoping the freedom we received in exchange would be worth the drastic downsizing our life would be forced to undergo. What I didn't know then is that living tiny was somehow about to create a bigger life than I could have ever imagined. This white school bus named Oliver changed my life.

What is Woke?

I'm not going to lie - we came back to the grid yesterday hesitantly. After a week of doing nothing but this, totally disconnected from the outside world, we were loath to leave it behind. We spent the week lying in this hammock, reading, and connecting over too many cups of coffee to count. We baked cherry pies we ate for breakfast, walked together in the ice-cold creek behind us, and had picnics that faded into watching the stars appear between the treetops. Mostly, we talked. A lot. About the world around us, what we've seen in our almost nine years together, what we're experiencing collectively now.

We felt into the situations and stories that have surrounded us the last few weeks. Brainstormed ways to move forward, places that light needed to shine and how to be a conduit for it. I think we are all looking at the world around us right now, then looking at ourselves and trying to discern our place in it. A hard enough task in a world not on fire, and an almost impossible one in the scope of our current climate, where no matter what you believe you will find vehement opposition telling you you're wrong.

Even so, despite not fully wanting to leave and knowing what we are coming back to, we came out of those woods with lots of ideas and plans and, above all else - hope.

We have a lot to share. We are, by trade, writers, and that's what we do here - we share stories. Some of those stories won't change. This is, after all, an account detailing the lives of two digital nomads living in a bus. But we have other stories to tell now beyond our tiny home. They are stories about this period of time and the world this little bus rumbles around in.

We hope you'll find value in them all.

(June 15, 2020)

I have to ask," he says, "What does the 'Since We Woke Up' on the side of your bus mean?"

We are at the only open tire shop in Cheyenne, Wyoming after blowing a tire thirty miles up the road and riding in on the massive tow truck that hauled our beloved skoolie, Oliver, here to have it replaced. He has a kind face and the open demeanor of someone who spends his life traveling from truck stop to truck stop interacting with strangers, and I sense no hostility from him.

Still, in the wake of the 2020 election season this is a loaded question, and I answer him carefully but honestly. "It refers to the point in our life when we actually took a good hard look at it, realized what was serving us and what wasn't, and decided to do more of the former and less of the latter. We sold everything we owned to get out of debt, have more freedom, and travel. We named our social media account Since We Woke Up to document everything that happened since that time."

"Ah, good, good," he says, laughing. "I have friends who said they woke up and the next thing I knew, they were Democrats!"

This book began on that social media, in the tiny squares of our Instagram account by the same name. The short captions that accompanied the photos of our life became the outline I expanded on to create the story you're about to read, the one about our journey of waking up and living life on purpose.

But, as that interaction proves, being "woke" has acquired an interesting status in our society, a trending idea that encompasses quite a few definitions depending on who you're talking to. That being the case, I think we need to define exactly what waking up means in the pages of this book. Context always helps. Someone rear ends you and you're flaming mad, until you find out they're on their way to the hospital where their father has just suffered a heart attack, totally flustered and panicked, and suddenly, everyone's understanding and calm.

So here's the context of what "woke" means, both as a global whole and to me personally. Let's start with what the business of being woke in our society means. I actually did pretty extensive research while writing this chapter and fell down a veritable rabbit hole of wokeness within different contexts, but I'll try to tidily sum it up in a few short paragraphs. Apologies for any additional levels of woke I don't include. I'm not a professor of social constructs, just a storyteller trying to set a stage.

Merriam-Webster defines woke as being "aware of and actively attentive to important facts and issues (especially issues of racial and social justice)". According to Wikipedia, the term, in this context, began as a derivative of the expression "stay woke", and refers to a growing and continuing awareness pertaining to social and racial justice issues. Before it became a staple of social media hashtags and apparel slogans everywhere, it was used mostly within these circles as a rallying call.

By the late 2010s, "woke" was adopted as a term used in association with left-leaning political stances, LGBTQ+ activism, feminism, and other socially and culturally liberal causes. If you were progressive on the issues, you were undeniably woke. And heaven forbid you didn't know what woke meant, in which case, you were obviously and decidedly not.

Then, ironically, the term was picked up by the political right and weaponized. Being woke suddenly became a label worn by pretentious hippies who believed they were better than those poor fools who were still fast asleep. Even further right movements co-opted it for themselves, filling chatrooms with talk of who the "real woke" ones were.

But the political arena doesn't have the monopoly on being

awake. Even before social movements and politics got all woke, religious and spiritual folks talked about the practice of spiritual awakening. In this context, waking up is a process, a journey from being asleep in the world to becoming aware of the infinite one around us and our connection to it. For the dogmatic and organized religious institutions, this of course meant waking up to your sins and shortcomings and dedicating your life to something higher and more profound.

In more spiritual circles, it mostly centers on a release of the ego that leaves room for a "higher self" to come through, or what the Taoists call a return to the original spirit. Spiritually awakened individuals are personally responsible for their actions and see them in the scope of the larger picture, where we are all connected. They don't follow the status quo or latch onto the momentary upsets of the world, letting their own internal compass and knowing guide them.

In other words, woke is a loaded word. But for me, and in regard to the moniker our social media, website, and even this book sport, waking up wasn't any of these things. Or rather, perhaps it was a little bit of all of them.

When we were in the planning stages of building the bus that would become our home, I decided to start a social media account and blog to detail the journey for those who cared to watch, which I assumed at the time would be mostly family and friends. I sat down to set it up and found myself staring at the blinking cursor asking for the username I'd like to attach to it for over an hour. This creative block led to a protracted conversation over the following week between Mike and I as we bandied names around. Our social media handle (and subsequently, this book) could have just as easily been named something boring that didn't need an entire chapter of a book to qualify it.

One night later that week, however, Mike asked me a question. "What will you show on this blog, besides the fact we're turning a school bus into a home?"

I responded, "Everything that happened since we woke up, I guess."

The next day, our account officially became Since We Woke Up. And now we've gotten that out of the way, let's talk about what that moment of waking up looked like for us.

During the political season of 2016, we found ourselves confused and disgusted. Yes, for just a minute here, politics enters this book, but we're not going to get all messy with it. For the most part, I don't allow politics to have much bearing in my day-to-day life, because there are just so many other more important things to spend all that caring on. But at this point in our story, for just the briefest of moments, politics mattered and played a pivotal role in changing the course of our lives as the motivator to get onto a plane and out of our own country for the first time. You see, with no good candidates on the ballot, in our opinion, and the general consensus around us summed up as "just vote for the lesser of the two evils", we decided instead to exercise our freedom by leaving the country and taking our first international vacation during the election. Some members of our family were flabbergasted by this choice.

"How can you just not vote?", they exclaimed.

"Your vote counts, it's a responsibility!", others said.

Mike would quietly remind them he'd already fulfilled a few other patriotic responsibilities, like serving in the military, and he hoped that would serve as an acceptable tradeoff for not voting in a single election, especially not one his conscious was torn over. For my part, I kept it short and simple – I will never make a choice simply for the sake of saying I did so to appease others, especially if it's something or someone I don't actually believe in. I will especially never choose between the lesser of two evils if I have the choice to create my own third option I do believe in.

And if there's one thing I absolutely believe in, it's travel. Which is how we found ourselves on a plane out of the country in the week before the election, headed to Italy for several more. By the time we returned the rest of the country would have made the decision as to who the lesser of two evils was and we would be fresh off a few weeks of beautiful art and food and music, reminded of what truly matters outside the political drama in our own country.

And that's exactly how it happened. We woke up one day to read we'd be coming home to a country now overseen by a former reality TV show host and then walked down the street to find a cappuccino and cornetto alla crema before meandering over to the Colosseum and Roman Forum. Life swirled on around us, oblivious to the political happenings and drama that blared from the front of every newspaper.

But something else happened on that trip that we weren't expecting. We woke up.

For the rest of my life, I will remember the exact moment my eyes truly opened for the first time. It was in the Piazza del Popolo, sitting on the stairs of the giant obelisk in the center. My mouth was full, the second pastry of the day melting on my tongue, a man blew giant bubbles for the children to chase, and vendors moved through the milling crowds of tourists with their trinkets as the warm autumn sun slanted down through the clouds in the way it only seems to in Rome. As my tongue captured buttery crumbs from my lip, I was thinking to myself I'd never been so content in all my life when Mike thoughtfully lowered the cappuccino he'd been about to drink.

"I think maybe we're doing this whole life thing wrong, Tawny."

That one sentence started the conversation that changed our lives. It would take a few years for the seeds planted that day to take root and bloom into the life we have now, and the growth period was full of hard and painful moments. We stood at the edge of bankruptcy, lost friends, worked ourselves into utter exhaustion, and weathered storms that bent us so low we thought we might break.

This book is that story. It isn't always pretty, and at some parts the telling gets a little rough. I had to backtrack into our individual tales, dredging up old emotions and memories, bringing them forward to help the present make sense. Although our social media and website have never shied away from the harsh realities and downsides of bus life, this book is, at times, a far cry away from the pretty photos you'll scroll through on the 'Gram. It's the real, gritty, sometimes painful story of how we upended the life we were told we should want for the one we actually did.

In other words, here's what waking up meant for us.

When in Rome

Rome. Photos, guidebooks, traveler accounts - none of it can adequately explain the sheer breathtaking beauty of it. It's as if God himself perpetually smiles down upon it in the form of the sunbeams that filter through the cloud cover.

It's everything I expected and then nothing remotely the same all in one - the smell of earth and damp always constant, cobbled streets crowded with people talking in six different languages until you step into the heavy arched doors of a church and meet with complete silence under the soaring frescoed ceilings, little Italian grandmas with head scarves stepping off the bus to yell at the driver to hurry as he loiters talking on the street at the end of the route, marble statues and fountains hidden around every corner and niche and teenagers making out on street corners - it's the most beautiful chaos I've ever seen.

(November 3, 2016)

As the story of our waking up began in Italy, it seemed appropriate this book should too. Italy captured my heart in a way no other destination has, and no matter how far we've traveled, how many beautiful places we've seen or experiences we've had, if you asked me right now to pick one place in the world to settle for the rest of my life it would be somewhere in that boot-shaped peninsula.

I wasn't born in Italy, but it's where this version of my life began. I've heard it said we all have two lives, with the second beginning the day we realize we only have one. In Sanskrit, they call an enlightened being a *dwija*, meaning twice born. When an individual is born, they grow and are raised under whatever customs and religion and politics and culture surrounds them, adopting characteristics and personas for themselves based on and out of those social mores.

Twice born means the individual reaches a point where they question the established norms they've been raised in and their place within this construct. Upon finding they have outgrown whatever personas they've adopted, they demolish them in order to be consciously reborn into a self more in line with who they truly are, albeit one that may now run perpendicular to the usual path.

It was in Italy I experienced that second birth, and it's that experience to which I always attribute my love of the country. But the truth is, I've loved Italy since the first time I saw it. And I mean that quite literally. As our plane dipped below the clouds and I saw the city of Rome spread out before me, I found myself crying. Mike touched my shoulder lightly and met my eyes with a questioning look, and all I could manage was, "I know this doesn't make sense, but I feel as if I've just come home." To this day, tears burn my eyes when I think about that moment.

I cried a lot that month to be honest. The first time I ate real Roman pizza, when I saw Michelangelo's David, in numerous churches along our path, at the top of Saint Peter's Basilica as the rain dripped through my hair and the city of Rome spread out in front of us, and as my face pressed against the airplane window so I could get one last glimpse of the country that had stolen my heart.

I have a hard time explaining to people how pivotal that trip was to our lives, how deeply and madly I fell in love with the sprawling fields and winding cobblestone alleys and hushed cathedrals and crumbling ruins, because how do you possibly describe the indescribable? As a matter of fact, this part of the story almost wasn't told except as a passing blip, because I struggled to find a combination of words able to accurately encompass the experience. My own verbosity failing me, I will instead simply say Giuseppe Verdi may have summed it up best when he plainly stated, "You may have the Universe if I may have Italy."

That trip changed my life. It changed my marriage, which I didn't know at the time was starting to fail under the strain of our day to day. And it changed me, irrevocably. We're told from the time we're born who we are and who we should be, but it was in Italy I found the first pieces of the woman I *wanted* to be. I discovered the truest parts of my nature there, and realized I wanted to say yes to so much more in my life than I'd previously allowed. It would be years and several more countries later before this process was fully realized, but at the grand age of thirty, the first threads of who I actually wanted to be when I grew up were woven into the tapestry of my life.

It was also in Italy I found the darkest parts of myself and my marriage, pieces crumbling as surely as the ruins we walked through. It's a sad truth how blindly you can go about your life, completely oblivious to the parts falling into disrepair. If you pulled your attention away from your routine for even the briefest of moments the moldering bits would be quite obvious, but daily life has a way of keeping our attention diverted. It took a rather large culture shock, removing myself from the country of my birth for the first time, for me to recognize I'd dragged quite a lot of baggage besides my checked luggage over there with me. The woman in the mirror of our apartment there was a stranger to me, and away from the constant demands of our business and family, I realized the guy sleeping next me was becoming one in many ways as well. Italy shook me awake from a stupor of routine and obligations to the life passing me by.

The conversation that started in the Piazza del Popolo

continued in little pizzerias and gelaterias down back alleys, on trains that sped through fields of flowers and past crumbling stone ruins, and over the thousands of miles of our flight back to Montana. We came home from that trip reborn, looking at our lives with fresh eyes. I remember walking up the steps of the three-story colonial we were restoring and pulling my suitcase into the front door. The late afternoon sunlight was slanting through the windows of my home office and its French doors onto the newly refinished wood floors, but it suddenly didn't hold the same appeal for me as when we'd left a mere month before.

Looking back now, I can see we had a life many would envy, the whole American Dream come true in living color. A beautiful home on a street lined with trees where everyone walked their dogs in the evenings and waved to each other. New car in the driveway, two kiddos who walked to their school a few blocks away every morning and afternoon, and a little garden in the yard where we talked to our neighbor over the fence each night as we sat on our back patios. We owned our own business (a gym) and managed our own schedules and while we weren't wealthy, we made ends meet and went to bed proud to have worked our way to this point in our lives.

Most of us are brought up to believe that a specific life path is the one that will bring us endless happiness and success.

Finish school, go to college, get a job and work your way up, get married, buy the big house, have some kids, buy an even bigger house, get the fancy new cars and the newest gadgets to fill it with, and then someday, retire and spend your golden years bouncing grandkids on your knees and enjoying life.

But even a gilded cage has bars, and when we returned, we could see them for what they were. What they don't tell you when they're spinning these tales of wealth and success and happiness is it all comes with a trade-off. We'd never really stopped to think about it until that trip to Italy, but in those weeks after, as we resumed our life and went back to our routines, it was all we could think about.

See, that big house and the new car and fancy gadgets all came with pretty fancy price tags to match. The truth is we didn't really own any of it, it owned us. We were practically married to our business to keep everything afloat, and as the business grew, so did our expenses and the time it took to run it. My brother, acting as our nanny, picked up our kids after school and took care of them while we put in long hours at the gym. We worked nonstop to afford our lovely house and its luxuries, which meant in a twist of irony we were rarely ever home to enjoy them.

And so our unhappiness grew. Even as the business expanded and new opportunities arose, our enthusiasm dimmed. I look back on this time now with such compassion for these versions of ourselves, remembering how we struggled to continue on in a life we'd outgrown and had no passion for. Our clients felt the difference and the gym began to struggle for the first time, becoming an ever more tedious burden that suddenly felt like a constant uphill battle.

The conversation that began as an abstract thought on a beautiful Roman day became a haunting vision neither of us could shake, too scary and far away to touch, too lovely and almost real to forget. Every day it preyed like a wild animal roaming loose in my mind, coming out to snarl and howl and gnaw around the edges of my thoughts when I'd recall those sun-drenched Mediterranean days. And almost two years after we left Italy, half a world away on a Montana winter night in our bedroom, we finally said the words to each other we hadn't been ready to verbalize that sunny day – I'm not happy, and I don't want to do this anymore.

It wasn't the first time I'd said those words. I'd first spoken them seven years before to my first husband, right before I walked out the door of the beautiful home we'd built together and into the unknown. I've heard a lot of talk around the number seven and its poignancy in our lives. The seven-year itch, where a lot of dissatisfaction takes place in a marriage. That our bodies renew themselves physically every seven years.

And my favorite, that every seven years we become a new version, emotionally and mentally, of ourselves.

I don't know if there's any factual evidence or truth for these hypotheses, but in my own life I can say this: I married my first husband and left him almost exactly seven years to the day later, shattering the life I'd built and running headlong into the wild unknown. And now, seven years after that, I was standing on the precipice of doing the same, ready to implode the world I'd carefully constructed around myself since then.

I'm not happy, and I don't want to do this anymore. We looked at each other, the words hanging between us. I know in that moment we were both weighing our options – the American Dream suspended on one side of a scale, security and comfort in our known world, balanced against the uncertain outcome of a fresh start. And then he smiled at me, and the decision was made.

Just like that, the next seven years started.

The Last Seven Years

He sings love songs at the top of his lungs, creates drawings so beautifully accurate they could be photographs, and moves weights that still make my eyes pop out sometimes.

I saw him for the first time almost a decade ago, fresh off a military base applying for a job at the gym I trained at. A few months of deadlifts and friendship later, he kissed me, and I knew I was screwed for anyone else. A month later we got matching tattoos, and a few more after that I walked through a forest in a white dress to where he stood at the edge of a lake and pledged to love him forever.

And I have. He's still larger than life to me, a strange conundrum I hope to never completely understand, a vegan yogi warrior who speaks poetry and soul while lifting to metal. I also didn't know back then the struggles we would go through, how many times we would almost lose each other to foolish pride and our own egos, or how beautiful it would be when we came out the other side.

I digress a lot when he comes up, but I refuse to only post photos of the bus for the likes. If this account is about our life, syrupy posts singing the praises of this man are going to be part of it, because without him, none of it would be happening.

(February 2, 2019)

Of course, before we get into what happened after that night I should probably rewind and refresh you on how we each individually got to that point. The people who know us from social media have always known Mike and Tawny as a single entity. But now I've mentioned my first husband, I should probably also mention Mike's first wife, and the paths we each traveled separately before we merged onto a single one.

Both of us were born in Montana and knew we wanted something beyond the Big Sky country out of life at a young age. That's where our similarities end.

Mike is grounded, an earthy Virgo who easily calms storms that sweep up around him. He believes in justice and honor above all, dives headfirst into situations most people run away from, and is hyper aware of the thoughts and feelings of those around him in a way that sometimes makes his own life painfully uncomfortable.

I, on the other hand, am the chaos that swirls around him. I flit from idea to idea, mercurial as the weather and just as likely to give you sunshine as a hurricane. My empathic nature makes me the most nurturing and loving companion you could wish for, but as Mike likes to say, life with me will never be boring and can be a bumpy ride at times. You're worth it, he'll add wryly as he smiles that serious smile that makes his eyes crinkle at me.

I was born into a large, somewhat convoluted family tree. I have six brothers and one sister, but only one of those shares both parents with me. My biological father spent most of my life in jail for various drug and alcohol related charges after my mom left him, taking my brother and I with her. When I was four, she remarried a man who had two boys and a girl of his own, and it was this family of seven I grew up in.

We lived in a small single-story cabin with three bedrooms and one bathroom in a little suburb of Montana's biggest city, not that it's saying much to claim that distinction in a state where whole towns sometimes sport double digit populations. My mother was an aide at our school and my father was a handyman who worked various jobs at different times in my life. We were far from wealthy, but my childhood was a mostly happy one.

Disaster struck when I was an eighth grader. It was the first time I ever saw my dad cry, the day they told us he had an aggressive cancer with a low survival rate. He was larger than life to me, a modern John Wayne action hero who never once made me feel as if I was an adopted daughter and not his real one. That day, and his tears, are burned in stark contrast in my mind to every other memory I hold of him.

I could tell you more about the two years that followed,

how I watched my strong father turn into a frail shadow of himself, but in the twenty years since it happened, I've still not managed to find words to encompass the crushing pain that time contained. My memories from those months are bleak – a stitched together family coming apart at the seams as the binding that held it all together slowly died in front of us. And he did die, when I was fifteen, after two years of transplants and crushed hopes and pain, surrounded by the family he'd created. I didn't know then it would be one of the last times the family I'd grown up in would be all together in the same room. Even if I had I'm not sure I could have appreciated it, all of us huddled around his tired frame, hands stretched out trying to hold onto him as his breathing became shallow and then ended on a final sigh.

My older siblings, his biological children, left home and moved away after that. My mom started seeing an old friend she'd reconnected with, and in the aftermath of my dad's death, my siblings' departure, and her newfound happiness, I found I couldn't take it and moved out myself. As an adult woman who's both experienced and caused pain, I can now see she'd spent two years watching the man she'd intended to grow old with slowly die and leave her alone, and she needed something for herself after dedicating two years to her grief and his care. And as it happens, it turned out to be a good thing for me that she did run headlong toward her own happiness, as the man she chose would one day become the father of my adult life after I grew up a little and got over myself, someone I would come to depend on and trust and love deeply. At the time, however, as an angry teenager who'd just lost her father and family in one fell swoop, I couldn't be near her without wanting to scream at the perceived injustice that was her following her heart instead of allowing her life to be a shrine to my dad.

That period of my life is murky and studded with terrible decisions. I moved out as I started my senior year, which meant I worked full-time to pay expenses while finishing high school. I started drinking pretty heavily and often, got into a terribly toxic and emotionally abusive relationship, and gave up on everything that had been important to me, like my lifelong pursuit of music. As I pulled away from my career dreams and people who loved me, I had only one goal – graduate and get as far away from my godforsaken hometown and its memories as possible.

And so, while the rest of my peers were heading off to their best laid college plans, I left Hollywood movie style, almost before the ink was dry on my diploma. I loaded up my old Saab hatchback, a few hundred bucks to my name, and drove all alone a few states over to where my latest boyfriend was starting pre-med in Washington. I planned to enroll in college for nursing and never look back at where I'd come from. Unsurprisingly, these hasty teenage plans didn't exactly work out, and a few months later I found myself in a strange city, broke, once again single, with a car that wouldn't run and about to be evicted from the dirty studio apartment I'd let when I arrived full of hope for the future.

It's at that moment a bright spot appears in my story, and his name is Evan. I took a job at the only place close enough to walk to, a Wendy's fast-food joint. I came in to collect an application, and I will never forget how his shy eyes widened when they saw me before refusing to meet mine again as he set me up for an interview with the hiring manager. A week later I saw him again from under the brim of my new crew hat as I was trained on the line. Blonde hair, blue eyes, and a crooked smile that made my young, hurt heart flutter every time I saw it.

He barely spoke to me for the first few weeks except to give me orders as the manager on duty, and in the end, it was another manager, his best friend, who dropped the hint that would hook us up. We started dating in February, moved in together a month later, found out I was pregnant in May, married in October, and welcomed our son, Aidyn, into the world almost a year to the day we started dating. The seven years of our marriage were mostly happy. We added a daughter named Ellery to our family, and I quit working to be a stay-at-home mom as he started a job at a bank. He quickly climbed the ranks to a supervising position that made more money than I'd imagined possible growing up in our little single-story house, and we sunk into life with his family, one more accustomed to the nicer things in life than my own.

Evan is one of those partners I wish everyone could be blessed with. Secure, stable, thoughtful, loyal to a fault. He has an insane work ethic, a wicked sense of humor that can diffuse just about any situation, and he pours himself into taking care of the people he loves. But we were oil and water in so many ways. I want to talk, constantly, about everything. Evan is quiet, and firmly believes bad feelings should be kept in little boxes in the back of our minds. That's a direct quote, not my words incidentally. I'm all fiery passion, he's calm waters. Once in a fight I swept an open can of pumpkin off the counter, where it swirled comically through the air, covering every surface of our beautiful kitchen in orange goo. As I stood boggle-eyed and steaming mad, daring him to respond, he flicked pumpkin off his cheek, looked around, and started laughing so infectiously it immediately ended the fight.

I can see now how it happened, how the disaster was there all along waiting. I was a broken 18-year-old, simultaneously yearning for a family to replace the one I'd lost while not allowing anyone close to me so I couldn't be hurt again. In hindsight, he never really had a chance, but his extreme love and my overwhelming need to have it kept us going. I threw myself into being the perfect homemaker, started a little online business selling dyed yarn and wool, and for a time, it kept me occupied enough I was able to ignore the nagging thought.

I'm not happy, and I don't want to do this anymore.

Right before our son was to start school, my mom started having extreme panic attacks that sent her to the emergency room. All the feelings she'd suppressed after my dad's death came roaring up out of nowhere years later, and as she worked through them (now with a new husband and two new sons added to the mix), it was decided we should move back to Montana to be closer to her. And so I returned to the city of my birth and all its memories, little family in tow. We built a house down the way from my parents, sent the kids off to kindergarten and preschool, and I started a career in fitness while Evan put his managing skills to use at a new company. The American Dream, version 1.0. And for just a moment, it absolutely was a dream.

Unfortunately, our beautiful new home became the stage for the final scenes of our marriage. I still take on all the blame, a broken woman returned to the scene of an earlier crime, both victim and villain, who single-handedly murdered this version of the future for her family. I'm being dramatic, of course, a long-standing trait of my Gemini nature, but it isn't too far off base to say I was the main problem in my marriage, and Evan fought for me to the bitter end. Unfortunately, I didn't see in myself a life worth saving, and so we played out our last lines in the failed production of our relationship. We went out to dinner for our seven-year anniversary a few weeks after we separated, both knowing it was the closing act in our mutual story, and then got into our cars and drove away to begin our respective individual ones.

I'm not happy, and I don't want to do this anymore.

Of course, the end of one act sets up the beginning of the next, and it's at this point the stage is prepared for Mike to enter, fresh from his own journey to that fated point in time. But I can't close the door on this chapter until I explain that Evan was, and remains to this day, one of the best men I've ever known.

If you follow us on social media, you know we now live as a blended family, parked part-time on a small homestead we're all building together when we aren't traveling. His love and unselfish nature kept our marriage together far longer than it otherwise would have lasted and is the foundation upon which the remainder of our story as a family was built. In the middle of one of the deepest pains of his life, he continued to love me and our children more than his own life and happiness. It allowed them to be raised in a manner which involved not only both their parents, but the man I brought into their lives a short time later, someone he could have loathed as an usurper but instead embraced like a brother. I've rarely met another person like him, and I owe so much of the happiness I eventually found in my life to his unique love. It's one of the greatest gifts I've ever been given, both as his wife and now, as his friend.

That's not to say I can't recognize now, from this healthier place in time, that I also had a hand in our current happiness. As I imploded my life for the first time, a healthy dose of guilt caused me to take half the debt and none of our assets in the divorce, meaning I lived in a car for a few weeks until I got on my feet and allowed our children to stay with him, coming and going from my old home like a ghost after they'd been tucked in and before they woke. We all have both regrettable and redeeming qualities, and I certainly tried to make up for the pain I caused in other ways. But it's important for me to definitively say that in this moment of the story, Evan picked up the shattered pieces of our lives and held them through his own pain in a way that would allow us to put them back together differently and create the family unit we are today.

And it's at this moment, one of the worst in my life, that I met Mike. His story leading up to this point isn't exactly a happy one either. And it isn't really my place to tell, but to understand the part he plays in mine you need to know a few basic things about it.

Mike left our hometown right after high school, just like me. He didn't come from a broken situation, but he had his own crosses to bear, his own points to prove. At the tender age of eighteen he went straight into the Navy and the BUD/S training program. He was ready – he wanted that title and the acclaim that goes with it, the chance to prove to everyone he wasn't just some poor kid who grew up in a trailer and wouldn't amount to anything. This chip on his shoulder plays a large part both in his own story and our mutual one, so it's important to know that the self-possessed man who lives in a bus with me today was once a scrawny kid from the trailer park who got beaten up and teased until he started going to the gym every day after school and became a man no one wanted to mess with.

Raring to prove himself in the world, he headed off to boot camp and the intense training programs that lay beyond it. However, once there, he learned he wasn't ready after all, and so during hell week he rang the bell and went to a new post on nuclear security. It was here he would meet and marry his first wife, gain a few ranks and the command that went with them, complete a few special training programs, and start cross-training with Marines, teaching members of both branches to fight. However, even with the respect of his commanding officers and those under his command, training across multiple branches, the chip on his shoulder would continue to scream, and so he began to train to go back to BUD/S for a second time. This time, he swore to himself he would be ready.

And physically, he was. It wasn't the work or hell week that got to him when he entered the program for a second time. "The first time," he always tells me, "I just wasn't ready – too young, too stupid, too full of my own ego to even think I might not make it, so that when I realized I wasn't ready, I just collapsed in on myself."

"The second time," he says as he shakes his head wryly, "my body was there but my heart wasn't anymore."

Behind the scenes of the grueling, physically demanding training days, his first marriage was ending in a messy divorce. And while he was at the top of his class physically, ready in a way he hadn't been the first time, the fire that once burned inside him for this dream was dying. One evening, mentally and emotionally strung out, he sat up all night with these two warring parts, the one who needed to prove something and the other who was ready to move on. This is your dream, he told himself, your big chance, you're at the top, don't blow it – except for the haunting thought that kept repeating.

I'm not happy, and I don't want to do this anymore.

Dreams change. Our desires change. Our needs change. Except Mike didn't fully grasp that who he was when he started the program and who he'd become in the interim had changed, which meant when he left his room the next morning to go ring the bell and resign from the program for a second time, decision made, he did so considering himself an absolute failure. Failed dreams, failed military career, failed marriage, and to his mind, a failure of a man. His worst fears confirmed, he left the military and his first marriage a hollow version of the person who'd shipped off to boot camp so determined and confident four years before. He was, he realized, what he'd always feared – just a piece of trailer trash who would never amount to anything.

This was the man I met.

He walked into the gym I trained at looking for a job, and it fell to me to help him learn the ropes. We got to know each other between client sessions and over workouts, and before long talking to him was one of the most anticipated parts of my day. As my world started collapsing behind closed doors, he was a constant I could depend on to make me smile. He had started dating someone as he left the military, but with the chip now a mile wide on his shoulder it was only a short time before his relationship was also suffering, and our mutual issues bound us together as we helped the other navigate the turmoil occurring in our respective relationships. He became my best friend, a rock I could depend on professionally and personally to help me make it through the day.

I can't tell you the exact moment I realized I was in love with him, a situation complicated by the fact that we worked together, I had just left my husband two weeks or so before, and while they were on a break, he was still trying to work things out with his girlfriend. Somewhere between the lines of a thousand casual conversations, however, an underlying current of emotion crept in that suddenly erupted one day in the gym office.

The change came the day he discovered I had moved out and was sleeping in my car. I will remember that conversation until the day I die, a casual one in the back office of the gym just like hundreds of others before. This one, however, had turned a little serious.

"Tawny, you can't sleep in your car alone, it's not safe."

"Mike, I can't stay there anymore. All Evan and I do is fight now and I don't want the kids around that. And I can't afford a place of my own yet, so this is the way it has to be. It's fine, I park in a safe neighborhood and never in the same place twice."

"I'll come stay there with you. I can sleep in the front seat or something. If something happened to you, I'd kill myself for knowing you were alone and not trying to make sure you were safe."

I remember laughing. "You can't do that. Rory told me the other day half the staff think you're in love with me, and we can't give them anything that would make them think it's actually true."

A weird, pained look came over his face and the air around us shifted with sudden tension. I remember reading once in one of the romance novels I used to steal from my mom's room that "the air was electric" between the heroine and her lover, and I suddenly understood exactly what the writer meant. In that moment, as I watched his body go rigidly still and saw the careful control it appeared he needed to suddenly exert over himself, I knew.

"Oh," was all I managed.

He looked at me with his deep chocolate eyes, intense and burning in a way I'd never seen before. "Tawny, if you don't want anything to happen, you should probably leave right now."

You're just out of seven-year marriage, I told myself. He's broken and you're broken, and this can't possibly lead to anything good, and you have two kids to think about – the litany of reasons why I needed to leave raced through my head as I stood frozen in front of the door. But a glimmer of dawning crept through the chaos of logic flooding my forward brain, a tiny flame unfurling somewhere deep in my belly as the unspoken truth written plainly on his features hovered between us.

And then I saw the matching flicker of hope on his face as he saw me hesitate. Something inside me clicked, and I reached behind me to close the door to the office, sealing off the noise from the gym beyond and locking us in a bubble removed from the outside world. In one step he crossed the office and had me in his arms. Nothing in those stolen romance novels prepared me for what I experienced that day. The way he shoved me up hard against a wall only to catch my head gently in his hands before it hit the ground as we went down in a tangle. How I was simultaneously on fire and drowning, chills racing up my spine. His fingers weaving into my curls and pulling my head closer, and the tears that rolled down my cheek as he caught my sob in his kiss. The way my body reacted was completely foreign to me, but as I broke away from that kiss, chest heaving, only one thought pounded through my brain.

I would follow this man through hell to taste that passion just one more time.

It never stopped, that passion. Ten years later, as I write this and look up to where he's working across the couch from me, the liquid fire still races through my veins and I find myself shoving the computer from my lap to lunge across the couch to him. I've stood on a castle roof top and watched the sun paint the sky as it set behind St. Peter's Basilica, snorkeled through crystal waters to witness underwater jewel-toned coral cities teeming with sea life, and climbed a volcano in the dim predawn to watch the sun rise over another in the distance — and he remains the most beautiful thing I've ever seen. For as long as I live, I can't imagine anything will ever hold more magic for me than he does.

Of course, passion runs both ways. A spark like that doesn't just ignite the tinder at the base of romance and dreams, it turns little flames of annoyance and offended sensibilities into infernos of rage. It's a good thing I was willing to journey into hell to experience that passion, because many nights I was in a personal one as our tempers raged out of control and led to fights ending as the sun came up. With time, we'd learn to temper that side of our intensities, curb our respective egos and funnel that fervor into our dreams and each other instead of screaming matches. I can say this with confidence; I've burned in more ways than one for the man who upended my life in a single kiss, but I would cheerfully endure every moment of searing agony for the delicious flash fire of emotions he can still ignite with a look or touch.

We've spent almost every moment of our lives together since that kiss. There was a brief period where Mike returned to the military and we spent three months apart. A few short months into our married life, he left me standing beside the tarmac as a plane carried him away from me and toward a place he could nurse an old wound. That chip on his shoulder, still screaming he had something to prove. He was asked to come in on an opt-in contract for a program based on his prior service and knowledge. It was an offer of redemption, the chance he needed to change the ending. Instead, he quickly realized he'd found something more important than poking at his scars, something stronger than his pride, something more painful than his perceived failures.

Almost three months to the day he'd left, he returned home and brought an entire airport terminal to a standstill when he ran down the stairs, threw his seabag down to scoop up the curly haired girl with shining eyes and a dog tag around her neck waiting for him, and kissed her senseless until the smiling crowd watching them disappeared entirely.

"I promise, I'll never leave you again," he whispered into my hair, as people resumed grabbing their bags and the world returned. "I thought nothing would ever hurt as much as ringing that bell, Tawny, until the day that plane took off and I realized it meant a life spent mostly away from you. I knew as soon as I left my heart would never be able to be in it, because I left it here with you."

I will never begrudge those three months of separation. It wasn't the ending he once dreamed of as a teenager, but it was the one his soul needed. He came home to me a new man, not the one he is today, certainly, but not entirely the tormented soul who'd left me either. He found the first small measures of peace in his realization and subsequent decision, a recognition he hadn't failed something meant for him, but rather moved beyond an old dream he'd pursued for all the wrong reasons. Since that moment we've worked together, gone to nursing school together, and built a gym and tiny home on wheels together. Twenty-four hours a day, seven days a week, we're almost never apart. People often ask us, "Don't you get sick of each other, living so close all the time?"

And the answer, quite simply, is no. If you ask him what the best part of his day is, he'll say almost every time, "Getting into bed at night with her."

For my part, all I can say is he is my home. The first time his arms wrapped around me in the office was also the first time I understood a person could be your country. The seed planted that day turned into roots now sunk so deep into the other no matter where our travels take us, together, we can be home anywhere on Earth. He's larger-than-life to me, a warrior poet who speaks magic into my soul and will likely remain, for the rest of my life, the most beautiful thing I've ever seen, brighter than those who surround him even in the worst moments of his own darkness.

Because even in them, he teaches me, inspires me. I was always afraid of the dark. As a child I used to pull the sheets tight over my head, choosing the stuffiness of the covers to the perceived dangers lurking in my room when the lights went out. Then I became a young woman and discovered night wasn't the only place darkness was found, and that human souls held shadows that far eclipsed the inky black of midnight. I developed caution, apprehensive and fearful of the murky recesses hidden within humanity and my own mind. And then I met him and learned the beauty that sometimes hides in dark places. I never feared the night or my own shadows again.

People used to think we were crazy. Our first tattoos for each other were inked on a month after that office kiss, and we were married a few months after that. We started and quit nursing school together to build our gym. We got up at 3:30 in the morning for years to be able to work out together before our day started. It's actually why we named our gym The Asylum — because people were always telling us we were nuts, and we joked we should build ourselves a little asylum of our own to house the crazy.

So when we announced we were buying a school bus, selling off everything we'd owned, and turning the bus into a tiny home we could travel around in, people just nodded their heads and went along with it. "That's just Mike and Tawny," they must have thought to themselves, "At it again with another crazy decision."

Two years later, the glimmer of an idea that began in a piazza in Rome became a solid glow on the horizon.

Satawny

Before a bus, fitness was our entire life. What we ate and what our workout was for the day and how we looked and how much we deadlifted were pretty much the most important things in life. And in all those scenarios, it was never enough. There was always some new diet, some new workout, some new goal, some way I could look better. While it was deeply satisfying to help other people reach their goals, I died a little bit every year personally because it was never enough.

I was never enough.

Part of waking up, for me, wasn't about selling off a lifetime of amassed "things" and finding what was really important. It was about realizing that I didn't have to base my entire identity around a job and lifestyle. That I didn't have to look like this to be of value. That, in fact, chasing this sometimes did more harm than good to my overall mental health. And that there was more to life than the four walls of a gym and selfies of my six pack.

Is this a derogatory statement toward fitness and those who prioritize it? No. Absolutely not. It takes hard work and a whole lotta internal fire to achieve what's in this picture, and I'm proud of myself and every other person who pushes themselves to be better physically. But for me, it reached an unhealthy point, where I didn't know who I was outside of fitness. Where I had no value if I wasn't deadlifting three hundred pounds.

Today, we carry a barbell and weights with us, and workout as we travel. For me, that means some weights and a lot of yoga. I've lost a lot of muscle. My pull-ups are no longer weighted. And that screwed with my head far longer than I care to admit. It still does some days, to be totally honest. Because how my butt looked in yoga pants was my largest concern for far too long, and it's hard to set down a decade of conditioning.

Sometimes people pick a barbell up to find and become a better version of themselves. I set it down.

Tawny two years ago would have told you the gym could fix almost every problem. Tawny today would tell you do what sets your soul on fire. If that's lifting weights, that's awesome. If it's selling everything you own and driving off in a school bus that's cool too.

Whatever box you've put yourself in, friend - don't be afraid to step outside of it one day and become something else. Something better. Something that looks more like you.

This doesn't look like me anymore. And I'm more okay with that every day.

(September 6, 2019)

Far and away the hardest part of closing that chapter of our life to start the next one was saying goodbye to our gym family. Because they were, family that is. Extricating yourself from an old life is hard enough when it's a wreckage, but what about when it's beautiful, with nothing wrong except it no longer holds any appeal?

After Mike returned from the military, somewhat at loose ends now he'd finally severed the last tie binding him to an outdated dream, he quickly enrolled in nursing school with me. We reasoned nurses were well-paid, able to take traveling gigs, and a skill set in demand no matter where you landed on the globe. Even back then, travel was something we yearned for. More than that, we'd decided it was time to get big kid jobs outside a gym. We couldn't just be gym rats for our entire lives, we decided, and medicine seemed like the next logical step up.

A year into working at the hospital, however, we instead realized we'd been on a far better side of the health spectrum (for us, anyway) working in the gym. Medical professionals work to fix health problems once the damage has already been done, their only option in many cases bandaging and managing symptoms of issues too far gone to ever be completely reversed. As trainers, it felt more like preventative medicine, working with people to create a healthier lifestyle devoid of preventable issues.

So we quit the nursing program to open our own gym. Tired of dealing with the larger gyms we'd trained for taking huge cuts of our training wages, and ready to train on our own terms focused on the individuals rather than how many training packages we'd sold that month, we figured it was worth the upfront investment to build our own space and business model.

The gym started in a pole frame garage we built in our backyard. Looking back, I can see how building that dream foreshadowed a much larger build and dream we'd take on almost five years later. Working twelve hour shifts at the hospital to continue to support our old lifestyle while spending every free moment and extra cent we had to build our new one, straddled mid-page between an old chapter and the next. The utter physical exhaustion of the constant push paired with the sheer emotional glee of building our dreams day by day. Months of chaos and juggling building toward the day the page would finally turn and we'd step fully into the next part of our lives.

And then, one unassuming day, it was done, just like that. We sent messages out to our old clients announcing we'd returned to the training game, and within the month we'd quit our jobs at the hospital to accommodate our packed schedules as old clients flocked back to us and new ones signed on.

Those early days were such a rush, waking up ahead of the sun to meet early morning clients before they headed to work and falling into bed at night massively satisfied after a day helping people meet goals. The gym had no boundaries back then, in our backyard, and clients floated in and out of our house, staying for dinner and barbequing with us in the backyard after training was over. Some of my fondest memories are from those hallowed days in our first year of business.

It was such a massive success, in fact, we soon outgrew the backyard. We had to consider bringing on more trainers when our schedules were too full to accept new clients, which led to us running out of room and equipment. The decision was made to lease a larger commercial facility we could expand into, and we celebrated our first year of business by moving to a large warehouse ten minutes away. Our clients showed up en masse to help us move the equipment to the new location, and then we all sat around eating pizza and designing the new space together. Over the next three years, our numbers would swell, we'd add new classes and trainers and programs, and The Asylum would become a safe haven for more than just that core group of people who followed us out of the backyard.

While the perimeter of the group would sway and flux, as new people arrived and old ones departed, the center would always hold firm, clients turned lasting friends who loved their gym and each other as much as we loved them. They brought us coffee and lunch, brainstormed ideas for new classes and events, volunteered their time to clean and staff, and generally surrounded us emotionally and physically with love every single day. This little ragtag group of our staunchest supporters and closest friends got us through every rough patch we encountered both professionally and personally, people of all ages and walks of life brought together by fitness.

I will forever remember and love each of those faces. They cheered each other on during classes, knowing when someone needed some good-natured ribbing to get their head back in the game and when a hug and a beer was the better course of action. They sweated together, cried together, laughed together, and more than anything, loved together. They participated in challenges to raise money for members in need and paid each other's training dues when jobs were lost or unexpected bills popped up. We had mimosas after yoga classes on Saturday morning to start the weekend off right and classes with especially heinous workouts written for each on their birthdays. They'd come in on lunch breaks or after work just to hang out, and the huge couch in the entryway saw more impromptu therapy sessions than the class floor saw burpees some days.

They dubbed us Captain Punishment and Satawny, the fearless leaders of their band. I stepped into the role with relish, famous for workouts that brought even the fittest to their knees in pools of sweat and chuckling as I added weights to the barbell between sets. They loved and hated me in equal measures, swearing at me when I yelled for one more rep only to hug me moments later as they crossed one of their goals off the wall.

It wasn't all about fitness, our gym. We taught them proper form when deadlifting and how to funnel their frustrations into the barbell instead of the people in their lives. How that push to get one more burpee than they did yesterday meant they could also push a little harder to get that promotion at work. That how they viewed their body directly translated not only to how they treated themselves, but others around them. Fitness was a platform we used to help people create the best versions of themselves not just inside a gym, but outside of it in their daily lives.

And they taught us too. Some of the lasting lessons I've carried on with me beyond the gym were passed onto me in that environment of camaraderie and goals. As a fun promotion, we once did an eight-week challenge culminating in a photo shoot for our clients. They spent two months working themselves harder than ever in order to reward themselves with photos of all their hard work. After weeks of waiting, the finished product was unveiled, and I was able to watch as client after client received and reacted to their album. The scenario played out almost identically every single time; the person would open the album with excitement and begin scrolling through. Looking over their shoulder, I would start pointing out the beautiful lines of muscle and perfect angles and shadows I'd noticed in each, celebrating their hard work. It was about this time each person would jump in with a "but". But look at that spot under my butt. But look at that cellulite. But see how my belly sticks out. But, but, but.

I was seriously taken aback. So much dedication and passion dissolved down to tiny perceived imperfections. I couldn't comprehend how they could see the images in front of them with anything other than appreciation. With the support of their gym family, however, each moved forward and posted their albums on social media, giving themselves the credit they deserved for having taken such a step out of their comfort zones, and I was gratified to see the comments of support and praise each of them received for it.

And then I got my own photos back. I was scrolling though happily, admiring my photographer's talent, when a closeup of my belly popped up. My heart sank and I felt the familiar sense of revulsion rise in my throat as I tried not to cry. The flash had highlighted something other than muscle – my stretchmarks, those silvery thin lines I've worn since my second child. The picture was, I'm disgusted and ashamed to admit, my worst nightmare, my flaws laid bare and enhanced under the glare of those lights and high definition.

Part of it was understandably justifiable. As a trainer I was, after all, held to a higher standard and scrutinized not just for what I could do, but what I looked like. My body was a walking advertisement for my business, and I can't tell you how many clients called me and signed on to train because they "saw me in the gym and wanted to look like" me. However, completely unjustified was the fact my belly remaining permanently marked in a way no amount of burpees would change was sometimes enough to send me into the fetal position, crying about how "ugly" I was.

This isn't an exaggeration, by the way – literally, the fetal position, arms wrapped around my head, great sobs wracking my frame and creating massive puddles of mucus and tears on my pillow. My patient husband would gently point out everything the body I loathed was capable of, how beautiful I was, how many clients admired it, and I would, in return, shriek it was because they didn't see all these hideous flaws clothes and good angles could cover.

This moment in time, as I sat staring in horror at the photo in front of me, was my first indication fitness could also be detrimental. Looking back, I can clearly see how working in the industry had begun to warp my perspective of myself, although it would take another couple of years before the full scope of the damage I'd inflicted on my psyche was made completely evident. I didn't realize it quite yet, but by then my entire self-worth hinged on how much I could deadlift and how defined my six-pack was. And in this case, was absolutely undone by a few pale lines subtly streaked across my flat belly.

So now I'm staring at this photo, almost throwing up, and I hear Mike vaguely through the tirade of self-hatred already starting in my mind remark how sexy I am, how much he loves my vascular arms and how awesome my tattoo looks, and I feel my anger rising (because how dare he try to make this anything other than the freak show it is) when I suddenly realize my rage is not for the loving man beside me – it's for myself.

I quite literally felt the snap in my brain as years of self-torment and despair flashed through it. I thought about every way this insecurity had disrupted my life and caused me to hold back or ruin precious moments. The time I'd watched everyone else frolic in the warm ocean while I'd stayed safely hidden under my cover-up, the sadness in Mike's eyes when I'd ask if we could turn the lights off while we made love, the compliments I'd thoughtlessly brushed off as I bemoaned the one part of myself I couldn't stop obsessing over. In that moment, every ounce of contempt I'd reserved for my flaws became centered instead on the voice in my mind that had been so loud for so long, screaming at me I would never be good enough or pretty enough or smart enough in light of this other *thing*.

As I felt that snap, as my mental computer rebooted, I found myself screaming back, "I DON'T F***ING CARE ANYMORE!", and suddenly, I was all alone in my head, leaving that loud mouthed self-construct, the twisted and dark side of Satawny, absolutely speechless.

A darkness I didn't know existed in me was suddenly apparent in the stunning light that followed. The years of self-deprecation and abuse faded away as I saw myself clearly, an image unfiltered by doubt and despair and hatred. I had a six pack, did pull-ups with a seventy-pound dumbbell attached to my belt, and deadlifted almost three times my body weight, but I'd somehow allowed those few small marks on my skin to overshadow those accomplishments. I spent my days lifting up and teaching other women to love themselves, and at the end of some of those same days you'd find me in front of the mirror crying about that sprinkling of flaws.

Because in our society, what was in that photo is ugly. We only want the beautiful, the perfect, no matter that it's fake. And so we stand at certain angles and flex just right and photoshop the rest and pray that no one will see underneath it all, we are all just insecure bundles of beautiful flaws. That night I taped the photo into my journal and wrote a reminder to myself beneath it.

"I almost started bawling when I saw this photo. And then

a dam inside me broke and I suddenly got very angry instead. With myself mostly, and the self-loathing I've subjected my poor body to for a decade, and then with our society, and its measure of perfection at the cost of our collective sanity.

Screw perfection. This is me. I grew two humans and it left a mark in a place other than my heart. You're so much more than a number on a scale or stretch marks or a size of jeans, Tawny my love. You're a soul. You're infinite. Of all the things you could be – is how you look the best of it? I hope not. You'll never be perfect. Be kind. Be brave. Be healthy. And be real."

Satawny wasn't real, not really. She was a persona I adopted, an alter ego I could step into who had all the answers, knew how to coax the best from people, and didn't have the insecurities and fears Tawny did. In some ways, Satawny was the best of me, a mentor and teacher my clients counted on. But she was also the shadow driving my inner critic, the source of toxic behaviors, a darkness I couldn't unsee now I'd recognized how profoundly deep it resided in me. I was simultaneously, however, afraid to let her go – what was I, after all, if I didn't have her? Who was Tawny apart from the deadlifting queen of The Asylum, devoid of her motivational speeches and lifting abilities?

When we decided to embark on bus life, it wasn't simply

selling a business we'd owned. It was saying goodbye to an entire community of people we loved. Leaving behind an all-consuming lifestyle built around the singular thought process that fitness was life. And for me, it was laying down the persona who was Satawny and admitting I was tired of the constant grind.

I didn't want to lift weights anymore. I didn't want to spend my life inside the four walls of a gym, my only goals to lift progressively heavier weights, always something to prove. I didn't want the image in the mirror to be any part of the measure of who I was as a person, let alone a major defining factor. I didn't want to be a woman so obsessed with fitness I forgot there was a whole world outside it, so worried about always looking a certain way I allowed precious moments to slip by.

And it wasn't only that. I was emotionally exhausted, depleted from years of striving to be everything to everybody at the cost of my own sanity and emotional wellbeing. Satawny was a fitness guru, a woman whose fire burned bright and hot enough to warm every single soul that came into her sphere, dazzling in her passion for life and ability to push others to new realms of self-worth. But I had been consumed in her inferno. Tawny was now little more than a pile of ash I drug home to bed each night, burned out by all Satawny gave away to others.

Saying farewell to our members and letting go of the haven we'd built was one of the hardest goodbyes I've ever experienced, as if I was ripping an actual piece of myself away instead of simply closing a business. But I realize now, I was. There wasn't room on the bus or in my life for Satawny, and I left her in the pages of that former chapter.

I do still carry her lessons with me, however. That most of the time, people just need someone else to believe in them in order for space to be held where they can begin to believe in themselves. How to know when someone needs a hug and when they need to be yelled at not to give up. That we are, all of us, capable of so much more than we realize. And mostly, that even the brightest parts of ourselves are capable of dark violence in their extremes.

It took me years of conscious work to find all the places that darkness still lingered in my soul, the places her message had been warped into hideous mantras of self-loathing and unattainable perfection. Painstakingly, like an archeologist sweeping away minute layers of dirt and time, I uncovered the wounds I'd been left with and carefully worked to clear whatever festering poison still resided in them until all that remained was the lesson. Slowly, little by little, I laid bare the darkness she'd never intended to impress upon my soul while pushing me to be better and replaced the shadows with the light she'd always imparted to others instead.

Those small pieces of myself I disliked warped over time into an all-engrossing focal point that dwarfed so much of who I actually was, throwing magnificent and undeserved shadows across the spectrum of my life and personality. Now being checked for the first time in my adult life since closing the doors of our gym, I find I'm staggered by the brilliance of who I am without those shadows, at the possibility I find there. And while leaving her behind was terrifying, not knowing entirely who I was without her, after all, it was also a relief to bid her and the constant striving she demanded behind.

I will always be grateful and humbled to have once upon a time been the woman they called Satawny, to have led such an amazing and inspiring group of people who loved each other so deeply. But I'm also so thankful to now live a slower, less goal-oriented life that requires I be no one other than myself. Satawny was a pretty rad chick, and some days I miss her voice in my head motivating me to get up and go pick up a barbell. But I've learned Tawny has her own brand of cool. There's a lot more pastries than pullups now she's running the show, and if there's one lesson I hope you take away from this book, it's that there should always, always, be more pastries in your life.

The Bus Conversion Begins

It's been months since we found Oliver and started this project. You haven't seen anything from us for a while because everything has fallen through. The sale of our house. The sale of our gym. Every single plan we had. All forward progress.

Oliver is sitting in the backyard, in exactly the same condition he was two months ago. Our house, the sale of which was going to finance this build, fell through three times over the summer. Our gym, the sale of which was our backup to the house and our ticket to freedom for traveling, fell through twice this fall.

We've been living with my in-laws for the last five months. It was supposed to have been one. Our hiatus from IG has been mostly during a period where we sat bewildered in our own lives, in the rubble of every plan we'd made that had crashed and burned, trying to figure out where to go.

"I haven't seen any posts from you lately," they say.

"Because I have nothing to post," I reply. "What am I supposed to show you?"

"The struggle," a wise friend replies. "Show them the struggle. The grit. The absolute fight to the finish line. That's more real than anything else you'll find on social media, and more of a comfort to the majority who will face the same uphill battle in their own struggle."

(A pause here: everyone needs this friend.)

So here it is, friends. The real deal. We're picking this IG and our blog back up. Instead of the weekly updates we'd planned detailing our progress, you'll instead be seeing this in between time where nothing is going according to plan. I'll tell the story later. The slow unraveling of all our plans, our complete dismay, the financial shit storm that came as we tried to juggle it all, and the slow climb back out of the pit we slid into.

(November 24, 2018)

Now to start with, neither of us have any construction experience. The sum total of it was the pole frame garage we'd built in our backyard when we first began our gym, which our construction friends had to come help us rescue when we couldn't get it to square up properly. Sometimes, looking back, I'm surprised we ever got it into our heads this was a project we had the skills and knowledge to complete. And yet, I'm so glad we didn't pause to question our ability, because in the end, scanty knowledge and non-existent skills notwithstanding, complete it we did. And this is always my first piece of advice to people considering a bus build. It doesn't matter where you're starting or what you're starting with – if we can do it, you can do it.

I'd seen bus conversions on Pinterest, but Mike wasn't interested. Remember, when this part of the story resumes, we know we want off our current life path, but are unsure of what the new one looks like yet. And bus life had a lot of unknowns that didn't appeal to Mike in the head space he was in at that time. He didn't want to trade one version of life he was unhappy in for a version featuring a dinky little apartment on wheels he was certain would lead to even more unhappiness.

One night, however, as we searched Netflix for our evening's viewing pleasure, a documentary called "Expedition Happiness" popped up. For those who haven't seen it, it features the journey of a young European couple who come to the US, convert a school bus, and then journey up through Canada and Alaska, down the West Coast, and into Central and South America. Even though he wasn't necessarily interested in bus life, what better show for us to watch, as we contemplated our own unhappiness, than one about the pursuit of it? And just like that, in the time it took that documentary to unfold on our television, Mike's mind changed. A short conversation later, we'd decided on our new course of action.

We would sell the business and our house, find online jobs that could travel with us, start homeschooling the kids, and turn a school bus into a tiny home. As if it was all just that easy.

I remember sitting in our king size bed that weekend making numerous planning lists – steps we needed to take before we could start, what to sell and keep, people to talk to – interrupted with excited laughs as we imagined how our families and friends would react to our newest hairbrained scheme. Our "crazy" was about to leave The Asylum, we chuckled.

I saved those lists, and they looked something like this:

1. Talk to the kids and make sure they're okay with this. Do they want to be homeschooled? Will they push themselves to learn when they don't have a structured class schedule? Are we prepared for the added responsibility? (Can we even do this? Will they even want to?)

2. Talk to Evan about what this means for our custody arrangement. Do we travel for a few weeks and then stay home for a few weeks? Travel by ourselves while he has them? FIGURE THIS OUT FIRST.

3. Figure out the logistics of life on the road. Where will we find water? Where will we park? Can we get insurance on a bus?

4. Figure out what our must-haves are and start planning to make sure it's all doable. What do we HAVE to have, and what can we live without? (Note: Mike says

no center aisle layout)

5. Talk to our gym members. Should we sell the gym? Close it down and sell off the equipment? ~~Will it survive without us at the helm, or would it better just to close it?~~ Don't just close it, try to keep it open for our little gym family. Hold a meeting and let them decide?

6. Find a bus. Has to have a DT466 drive train, at least 70 passenger (the longer the better), flat nose, and be fresh off a school route. (Check Craigslist, Facebook, eBay, etc.)

7. Get house ready to sell and list (see house list).

8. Sell off all items we won't need (see sell list).

9. Talk to dad and ask if he can help with the technical components – metal work, plumbing, propane.

10. Talk to Levi (my brother) and ask if he can help us figure out the best sized solar system for our needs.

11. Don't forget you can do this – you built the gym, and you can build this next chapter too.

I'm sharing these little details here because sometimes on our social media, people see the finished product and forget we were once starting right where they currently are in their dreaming – in the middle of the questions and uncertainty and seemingly never-ending and insurmountable to-do lists. We turned our lives upside down to build our beloved little skoolie, and while making the decision to chase our new dream was easy, seeing it to fruition was anything but. When I read back on these lists, I see us weaving the little cocoon of our new life around us, the space in which our idea would take shape and grow and evolve until it was ready to emerge into reality. I can see our doubts and fears intermingled with our hopes and plans, and it delights me to remember our younger selves hunched over these lists, planning the life we live today.

But while we were drunk on possibilities, the doubts were indeed large enough to quickly sober us up. How could we do full-time bus life with shared custody? What if the kids didn't want to do it, or hated it once we'd started? What if after selling everything and upending our entire lives, we found it wasn't for us? And it's a good thing we took time to think all these things through, because if we were asking ourselves these questions, we could bet everyone else would be too. And they absolutely did, worried for our happiness. From the outside looking in, our life looked pretty damned charmed at that time. A young couple with a beautiful home and successful business, leading their little gym family to better health, raising two humans in an environment of crushing goals and camaraderie.

We answered these questions, both for ourselves and others, with a single, all-encompassing reply – if we never try, we'll never know. And so, while the questions raged on (both in our heads and in conversation around us) we began working our way through that list.

Evan took our decision in stride and said we could figure out a way to make it work. The kids were more than happy to leave traditional school and try something new, and the idea of traveling and living out of a school bus was an adventure they were excited to try. My dad and brother signed on to help us as we needed it, and our gym family rallied around us and agreed the gym should stay open and new owners should be found.

And at first, it was easy. Within a few weeks we'd spruced up the house, ready to be listed right as spring came to Montana. After just a few days on the market, it went under contract and we began the process of selling off almost everything we owned. One of our trainers decided to buy the gym and the community tucked in around her, excited to see her step into her new role. For a few weeks, it appeared everything was just falling into place.

Including the bus.

During this period we found the perfect bus, a 2004 International RE with low mileage and our preferred drive train and chassis, fresh off his job hauling high schoolers around for the small city of Polson, Montana. One of our clients at the gym was a diesel mechanic for a school bus dealer who took it in on trade, and we snapped up our dream bus for a cool five grand.

House and gym pending sale, possessions pared down to the bare necessities, kids settled into homeschool, and bus purchased, we moved in with my in-laws and dove headfirst both emotionally and financially into the conversion. Within a few months our loose ends would be tied up, the bus would be done, and we would be on the road.

And that's when disaster struck.

Two days before our house was supposed to close, they discovered in underwriting the buyers had committed tax fraud and as a result, they lost their financing, causing the sale to fall through. In the same week, our trainer's father had a sudden heart attack and passed away. With her mother all alone on the family ranch, she was forced to back out of the gym purchase in order to step in there. In the space of a few days, our entire situation changed.

The story gets a little dark here for a moment. You see, believing the end of our financial obligations to a mortgage and gym to be at close at hand, we'd thrown our entire financial weight into the bus. When both deals went simultaneously upside down, we suddenly found ourselves caught financially between our old life and the one we were building. All bus progress had to halt immediately as we were forced to pick management of the gym and our mortgage back up, a task made harder by the fact that gym membership had begun to dwindle in the transition period. Barely breaking even now, it was all we could do to keep the place afloat, let alone cut ourselves a paycheck.

For six months, the bus sat half-finished in the gym's backyard as we struggled to make ends meet. Meanwhile, the gym limped along as we searched for new owners willing to step into a business not performing anywhere near as well as it had the previous years. The core of our little community rallied around us, but it was barely enough to keep the lights on. Our house, still sitting vacant on the market after having to be relisted, was broken into by some neighborhood teens. They had a party, trashed the staged furniture, and spray painted the walls and floor of the garage. The lingering haze of pot smoke amid broken alcohol bottles and smashed furniture was bad enough, but the spray paint also got into the outlets in the garage, damaging the entire electrical system. We had to borrow money from family to restore the house to a sellable condition, and by the time we got it cleaned and fixed, more precious weeks of the selling season had passed.

Our lowest point came one day as we prepared to leave for the store, and I told our daughter to go put on a different pair of shorts that fit her. She responded she didn't have any. A quick look through her drawers showed me she spoke the truth. Upon closer inspection, I noticed both kids' drawers were looking a little sparse on clothes that actually fit them.

"Why didn't you tell me?" I asked them, sorting through drawers. "If you need clothes, you have to let me know so we can get you new ones in the right size."

She looked at the ground and softly replied, "Because I know you and Mike are having money problems, and I didn't think we could afford new clothes."

In that moment, my heart broke. Not just because my young teenage daughter was aware of our financial issues and had decided to continue to wear overly small clothes rather than stress our budget, but because she was right – we couldn't afford them. Savings drained, debt maxed out, and checking in the red, there was no money for new clothes.

In the end, however, the kids truly needed them, and so we pulled out an old coin jar from the laundry room we'd had for years. Once cashed in, we were able to put together just under $100, enough to buy them each a few new outfits and undergarments in the correct size.

That night, after they'd thanked us profusely for their new clothes and headed off to their bedroom at grandma's house, Mike and I got into the shower. I remember sinking to the floor, completely despondent, tears running noiselessly down my cheeks as I wept hot tears of shame. Our situation seemed completely futile. We were flat broke, exhausted from trying to bail out the sinking ship that was our business, existing on the kindness of family, and now, I'd had to literally scrape the bottom of a coin jar just to provide a few necessities for our children. Bankruptcy seemed our only option, and in that moment, sitting in my mother-in-law's shower, I gave up.

Now when I say I gave up, I don't mean the throw your hands up in the air with an "oh, well" sigh kind of scene. I mean I checked out. Hard. Steam swirling around us, water running over my head and down my sides in rivulets, I left my body lying on that shower floor and floated up and away. I vaguely registered Mike saying my name over and over, but responding didn't seem to be an option. I heard his voice, I saw my body, but in that moment, I was paralyzed with fear and grief, beyond answering. Hovering over the form of the woman below me as if I was a bystander in this nightmare instead of somehow actually dislodged from my own life, watching him try to rouse her from the noiseless sobs that wracked her limp frame, I remember wanting to comfort him. But even his terror couldn't pull me back from my own. In the end, it was his tears mixed with mine that drew me back, as he wrapped his arms around me and whispered in a cracked but determined voice, "I will fix this Tawny. I promise, I will fix this."

A fierce promise, impassioned plea, and desperate prayer, he repeated it over and over as he rocked me, and I slowly sank back into the body of the woman he held.

The next day he called his sister, who owned a pizza shop, and asked for a job delivering pizzas. From then on, every night after the gym closed, he would run pizzas all over town, bringing home his tips and small paycheck to add to our struggling bank account. When the kids weren't there I went with him, and we tried to pretend it was an adventure instead of an act of survival. But at night, as he laid there staring up at the ceiling, I knew the old chip on his shoulder was aching. Failure, it screamed. You're a failure. You couldn't provide for your family, and now you've sunk from a business owner to a pizza delivery boy just to make ends meet. He carried the anguish stoically, a veteran of his own shame by this point. But it was palpable to me, his despair. While that additional income kept us simply teetering on the edge of financial ruin instead of going over, I knew it was only a matter of time until Mike physically and emotionally burned out. We needed a new plan.

I will pause to say we learned a lot, however, in that place, our rock bottom. They say when you hit it, there's no place to go but up. But we found out not only does rock bottom have a basement, it also doesn't have lights or heat and you can spend quite a long time stumbling around in the dark and cold looking for a foothold to help you head back out. While we staggered our way around, feeling through the blackness, we learned to hold onto each other in a way we hadn't previously known. What was actually important, and what wasn't. What we could survive, with no other options. As a matter of fact, I always say our first lessons in bus life started during this time and prepared us for the hiccups we'd experience on the road. It's hard to trip up a person used to jumping hurdles.

Those months are among the worst in our respective lives for the demons we each had to fight. Mike, faced again with his own perceived failures as a man. I, a near feral woman terrified of a cage trapped in a situation of her own making. But Mike's unwavering bravery as he once again confronted his worst fears made me want to be strong too. He and I always say we're at our best when the other is at their worst, and as I watched my husband set down his pride for the sake of his family, I found myself picking my determination back up and dusting it off. I looked back into the fire that had so recently consumed me and, with grim resolve, marched headfirst back into the flames. It was time to find a new path through them, and with Mike busy keeping food on the table, it would need to be me that forged it. While he worked those delivery shifts, I researched and made calls and ran the gym and hustled to find our next steps forward.

Our big break came when we took our house off the market. All thoughts of selling it aside, we instead rented it to a woman I'd gone to school with. She wasn't quite in a position to buy it, but she loved our previous home, and we were able to work out a rent to own contract. With the monthly mortgage payment off our plates and no longer a concern in our immediate budget, the smallest bit of breathing room was given to us and in it, we realized we could refinance the house to the same end as selling it. The equity tied up in our old home was enough to fund the remaining bus build and have enough left over to almost pay off our debt.

In this better head space, we also came to terms with the fact we were trying to keep the gym going for nostalgia's sake alone. It was a better financial decision to simply close it and sell off the equipment. The decision was painfully hard to make, and saying goodbye to our most diehard and longest running members will always be one of my most bittersweet memories. Good lord, but I loved that little ragtag group of people who stayed with us to the bitter end. They gathered around us for one more Saturday class, and then we walked out together and closed our doors for the last time. We sold and donated most of our equipment to a new facility opening up for military veterans, keeping just what we would use while traveling, and added the funds to our build budget.

I will never forget the day the equity check hit our bank account. Two months before all hope seemed lost, bankruptcy imminent, and I'd literally dug coins out of a jar to buy clothes for the kids. Within the week we were almost completely debt free, our credit score jumped into the 800s, and we had the money we needed to finish our build. Mike was able to quit delivering pizzas so we could get back to working on the bus, we rented a small apartment close to the gym, and suddenly, there was light for the first time in months. I cried again in the shower the night we moved into the apartment and started the bus build again, but this time it was tears of gratitude instead of fear swirling down the drain with the water.

At this point in the conversion, we'd gutted the interior, tinted the windows, and installed insulation and flooring, and it was in this condition it had sat all winter long in the backyard while we cried and delivered pizzas and waited for the tides to turn in our direction once again. As winter faded into spring, both around and inside us, we pulled open the doors for the first time in months and walked up the stairs onto the plank flooring. Forty feet of possibility spread out in front of us, the sun filtering in through the full banks of windows, he reached for my hand and we stood in the warmth together, ready to start the next chapter in our story.

The Conversion Process

This is our skoolie, Oliver. Oly is a forty-foot, 84-passenger 2004 International school bus. He was part of a trade in deal from a small town in Montana to a large truck retailer that we found completely by accident while looking at another bus. He has a DT466 engine with an Allison 3000 behind it.

We spent months waiting for him to come in once we knew he'd be available, because that drivetrain was worth waiting for. He has a black pirate logo on his front driver panel that we painted back on after his initial paint job, an homage to the high school he worked for.

We found $2.36, numerous candy wrappers and a plastic cross necklace when we cleaned him out, and he has a small ding on his rear passenger panel. He's about a month away from completion at the moment, and every time I walk onto him, I fall a little more in love.

(February 19, 2019)

I want to preface the breakdown of our conversion process with a little side note, and that is this: there is no one way to go about turning a school bus into a tiny home. Skoolie conversions span vast scales in terms of budget and features, and none is really better than another, in my opinion. The best school bus conversion is the one designed for your lifestyle and needs, that fits your budget and idea of "perfect".

For some people, this means the works – a raised roof, hydraulic lift system, extensive solar and water systems, and interior finishes that rival traditional homes. At the other end of the spectrum, some people choose to go bare minimum, leaving the bus mostly as is after the seats are out and adding base amenities that allow them to live and travel. Between those two extremes, you'll find thousands of builds trundling around the world in all styles, sizes, and levels of "done-ness".

You'll also find many different ways of going about the process. Some people hire their build out, relying on a tiny home company to create their vision. Others do the entire conversion themselves, or self-convert. The rest do some combination of the two, hiring out jobs they don't know how to or don't feel comfortable completing and finishing the rest of the build after. Even with our limited construction experience, we knew we wanted to self-convert. The idea of building our future home together coupled with not having to pay labor costs for someone else's sweat equity on our behalf was an attractive prospect. On top of that, as both my father and brother were RV techs, we had a safety net of sorts, knowing they could be relied on to teach us and fill in the gaps as we went.

One of the lists we created in those early planning stages included our build "must-haves", complete with a first rendition of our floor plan. Mike had only one big request – he didn't want a center aisle layout. While many builds utilize them to keep the walking space all in the tallest area of the bus or ensure an even distribution of weight, he wanted a design that didn't offer a straight view back to the bedroom. My list was a little more extensive.

I knew I wanted the kids to have their own bunks, and more than that, I wanted space between their area and ours to ensure we would each have some respective privacy. Many traveling families with younger kids can get away with having all the beds grouped together in one area, but with young teens on my hands that wasn't going to work. In order not to traumatize us all, better to make sure we all had areas of our own that could be closed off from the others. I also wanted a larger bathroom with space for a washer/dryer unit, a built-in eating space that could double as a desk for the kids, and plenty of storage. Mostly, I hoped to design a plan that was open and offered multi-use areas and features.

I can't even explain how much research occurred in those early weeks and months. Once we'd made the decision, we first had to decide what type of bus we wanted. Dog nose or flat, engine and transmission combos, length and passenger count, front engine or rear – there are a lot of factors to consider. After hundreds of hours spent on forums and reading through articles, we decided on a pusher (rear engine) with a DT466 engine and Alison 3000 transmission. Not only would it be affordable to work on and easy to find a mechanic for in the event of a breakdown, we felt confident this drive train would mean we weren't slowed to a crawl when it came to hills and mountains.

When deciding how large a bus you should get, it's a matter of space against maneuverability. A bus meant for twenty passengers drives much more easily than one meant for eighty, but the trade-off is a drastically smaller living space. Because we had two teens to consider, we knew we'd need all the space we could manage, even if it meant driving a bigger beast around.

We actually had a different bus in our sights when we found Oliver. Two buses were coming in on the trade deal, and it was the other we'd decided was perfect for us. When we drove onto the lot that day, we went straight to it, the bus we'd been staring at pictures of for weeks waiting for it to arrive. Unfortunately when we walked in, something just didn't feel right. Or rather, neither of us felt anything. It was entirely anticlimactic. Where we'd expected some spark of recognition, at least, there was nothing. Sensing our hesitation, the salesman asked if we'd like to see the other bus just for kicks. They were nearly identical, an inch or so in headroom the only difference (and the reason we'd picked the first), but as we entered the second bus, we both felt a little tug and a look passed between us. Later, he would tell me the second one just felt like it was meant to be our home, a rather odd statement for a person entering a school bus to make, but I understood exactly what he'd felt.

A few hours later, paperwork complete, we drove that 2004 International off the lot and out into the world. Our parents took a ride around the block with us when we brought it home, bemused neighbors waving as we drove circles through the neighborhood. Every year, my mother-in-law reshares the memory on her Facebook – a small sweatpants-clad woman with a messy bun and flip flops at the wheel of a ginormous school bus, looking back with a huge smile on her face as her husband hails her perfect right turns and the neighborhood swims lazily past the windows. If she'd known then of the emotional and financial hurdles they would face in the next year, her smile might not have been quite so wide that day. But every year it reminds me of how I felt in that moment, which was absolutely and unequivocally free. Our bus life was beginning.

Whether you're looking at a build on a budget or going all out, most conversions contain the same basic elements. First, there's the deconstruction. Having now fully dismantled a school bus down to the bones, I can tell the parents out there one absolute truth – your child is riding in a veritable tank. As anyone who has participated in this process can attest, every single part of deconstructing this bus was absolutely obnoxious due to the extreme number of bolts and rivets and screws and glue that hold it all together. It took us a week of arduous labor to strip it down to basic framework.

Removing the seats was step number one. Each is bolted through the floor, meaning one person had to work outside while one worked on the corresponding bolt inside. Many were so rusted they wouldn't turn at all and had to be ground off instead. The longer your bus is, the more seats you have to contend with; ours had fifteen on one side and fourteen on the other, and almost every single one put up a monstrous fight to stay in place. The final seats were the front two on the passenger side. For over an hour we tried every single tool and idea we could think of to pry the first one loose, but it held like grim death to its place of pride in front of the door, even after grinding through all the bolts. It was as if that seat was magically adhered to the frame. Finally, ideas and patience at an end, Mike braced himself against the only remaining seat behind it in frustration and heaved against it leg press style.

We have a saying in our family we use to describe

something getting broken in the process of normal use, "Miking it", a tribute to the sheer number of things he's destroyed while using them exactly as intended and not understanding his own strength. Examples of this include three different slide-style phones he slid right off their base while opening them, huge metal bolts snapped while he was hand-tightening them putting together weight racks, or the time he accidentally broke down a deadbolted door with his shoulder because he was moving so quickly, he took it for granted the door would be unlocked when he barreled through it. We sometimes joke it's a wonder he hasn't broken me, but for a man who has accidentally ripped bath towels while drying his back, he also possesses a level of gentle gracefulness that's completely at odds with his brute strength. Once again, however, I'm digressing.

This predilection for destruction does have some benefits – for instance, in this battle of wills with a seemingly immovable school bus frame. Mike's face turned red, the metal screamed and popped under the strain until, with a final shriek, it tore free from the floor and shot forward into the stairwell. With his entire weight behind it and nothing to stop him, the momentum carried him along with it and he rode the last stubborn seat down the stairs, nearly impaling himself on one of the legs as they tumbled out the door together. And thus, the production of removing bus seats ended with a dramatic finale.

The floors followed the seats. As the laminate and rubber and pieces of wood subfloor came out, so too did the detritus of over a decade of young passengers. Lodged in nooks and corners, we found $2.36 in coins, a clear plastic cross on a tangled necklace string, various small toys, and enough candy wrappers to start a bonfire. We also discovered littles notes, written in surreptitious places on the walls and floors once hidden by seats – JT loves MB, Mrs. Warner sucks, 4:20 rulez. Like archaeologists on the trail of some prehistoric culture, we uncovered the remnants of our future home's past, plucking up the treasures and adding them to a jar on the dash, wondering aloud what the unfortunate Mrs. Warner had done to warrant the angry epitaph carved into the wall and if JT still loved MB. To this day that plastic cross necklace sits in our bus, and every so often I run my fingers over it when I pass and smile.

The floors had a few spots with serious rust issues. When looking for a bus, checking the undercarriage for rust is a must, although you'll rarely find one spotlessly clean. We knew we'd be facing a few rusty areas around the wheel wells, and we considered scoring our preferred drive train well worth the time it would take to correct the problems before we began the job of building our home on top of it. My dad, metal worker extraordinaire, helped us get rid of the worst spots before welding reinforcements and new sheets of metal in place. We used hundreds of pennies to cover the small holes left from the seat bolts, and then sealed the whole shebang with Rustoleum.

Working up from the floor we came to the walls and roof. Many people choose to tear out the metal wall, ceiling panels, and the insulation behind them and start right at the exterior metal, but we decided to skip this step and build over them. After all, as we were still putting in insulation of our own, we figured it was just a double layer of insulation at the expense of a few extra inches of width. Others still remove windows they won't be using and skin over those spots with metal or replace them with RV windows instead. We didn't do either of those things, wanting to retain the look of a school bus from the outside. Instead, we resealed the original windows, added a special tint that offered both privacy and thermal protection, and then put black cardboard in the windows we'd be covering, so they would look the same from outside even once we'd insulated over them inside.

Last on our deconstruction docket was the tough stuff – removing the built-in bus heaters and corresponding pipes along with the myriad of electrical wires running from the front panels to the engine in back. We spent hours poring over diagrams we'd found online, identifying which colored wire went to which system, whether it was safe to pull or needed to stay, and painstakingly extracting the ones no longer necessary from the ones still needed. We hit a spot of trouble when we inadvertently disconnected the emergency hatch failsafe. As a precaution, all the emergency exits on our bus were wired to prevent the bus from starting if even one of them is unlatched. Realizing this could lead to issues while traveling and was more of a nuisance than helper for us, we set to work figuring out how to turn our little accident into a positive and circumvent future issues. It was the first of many such small missteps turned grateful discoveries we made along the way, and we learned another lesson that would serve us well in bus life – sometimes seemingly terrible situations offer us lessons and rewards if we choose to frame them the right way.

It took us hours of time and stress to trace our electrical system and discover why the bus would no longer start thanks to the tripped failsafe. But within that frustration and seemingly wasted time, we learned more about our bus and its systems, found a potential future headache for ourselves, and fixed it throughout the whole bus so it couldn't cause a problem down the line. Further, we learned another lesson in exactly what we were capable of if we only applied ourselves.

This mentality we cultivated during the build, that we shape our experience based on our perceptions of the situation and not the situation itself, changed our entire lives. We encountered so many setbacks and accidents. When we allowed ourselves to get frustrated or angry or upset, the outcome was nearly always negative, or a grudging "well okay then, at least that's done". When we instead chose to reframe the moment and approach the situation with a "what can I learn here" mindset, we always came away from it feeling grateful and calm. And this doesn't just apply when converting a bus into a tiny home. By implementing this principle in every area of our lives, from our relationships to business to parenting to menial tasks, monitoring our perceptions makes a dramatic difference to our daily lives.

For instance, a few years back while traveling with friends, our flight ran late and resulted in a mad dash from one end of the airport to the other to make our connecting flight in time. As if the task wasn't already difficult enough, we were returning from an international trip and had to reenter customs, meaning collecting our bags and rechecking them. We'd also already been traveling for well over twenty hours and were all exhausted and ready to be home. Our friends' bags and mine came out, but Mike's got stuck in the chute. With only minutes remaining before our flight was to depart and our very stressed-out friend getting more and more panicky, we told them to go without us and catch the flight, in case we didn't make it.

Ten minutes later we stood at our gate, panting and

exhausted, watching our ride home get ready to leave without us. Our friends were onboard, along with my purse, which they had been holding for me in the chaos. We were in a strange city late at night, with no money or identification or phone or transportation. As the plane taxied down the runway and we explained our plight to airline personnel, Mike squeezed my hand and winked.

"Well, Tawny, what adventure do you think awaits us here?"

One little perception tweak was the difference between being stranded in a major way and an exciting plot twist with a bonus adventure. And we ended up enjoying ourselves immensely. The airline staff, pleased and relieved we were taking this setback in stride, arranged for a hotel and transportation free of charge for the night since there were no more flights out that day. They also gave us money for dinner and breakfast and changed our flight back home to a better one. In effect, we enjoyed an extra day of vacation and a free date night, arriving home the next day in refreshed and renewed spirits.

Once home, we learned exactly how large a gift that missed connection ended up being. Our friends, who'd celebrated being able to catch the flight while feeling terrible we'd been left, rode the remaining three hours home only to circle the airport and end up diverted another hour and half away because weather wouldn't permit them to land. Already a late-night flight arriving home near midnight, by the time they taxied into the new airport it was the wee hours of the morning. Because it was due to a weather issue and not a fault of the airline, none of the passengers were given accommodations or a credit toward one, so they had to choose between renting a room out of their own pockets or kipping at the airport. The new flight was scheduled for early in the morning, meaning no matter their choice, they'd all have only a few precious hours before they were filing, cranky and groggy, back onto the plane. In the end, they arrived home mere hours before us, completely exhausted from the ordeal and already in need of another vacation.

I could literally fill pages of this book with similar examples of how framing our perception of and reaction to situations created an opportunity for us instead of the initial outcome we feared – wrong turns and roads that led us to amazing destinations we might have missed had we gone the right way, setbacks and delays so frustrating in the moment ultimately turned into blessings when we found a better solution during the wait.

Suffice it to say, this lesson we learned while preparing the foundation of our future home served us over and over again during the build process, and continues to this day to be our go-to coping mechanism for how we deal with stress and setbacks. When you ask yourself, "What can I learn from this situation and how can I change my perception of it in order to learn that?" instead of ruminating on the unfairness of it all and how it's going to ruin your day, you'd be surprised how many seemingly bad situations are actually adventures in disguise.

Over a month after we started, the bus was a hollow shell, ready for the build. Insulating and installing the flooring was first up, a fairly simple task compared to many others we would be undertaking in the following months but one that packed an incredible impact. When we finished the job and turned back to look at our work, what had been an empty metal tube on wheels the day before was now two hundred and fifty square feet of living space. Just like that, before plumbing or electrical or walls, we were in our future home. Of course, as you've already read, it's also somewhat ironically at this juncture our progress came to a grinding halt and we were forced to take six months away from the project.

From then on, however, work on the bus was slow but steady and we finished the remainder of the build in just a few short months. Every day, between clients and classes, you'd find us behind the gym, building our home. We framed the walls in preparation for insulation, electrical, propane, and plumbing, an easy job since there was only one real "room" in the whole floor plan, the bathroom.

After the technical systems were in place, we closed the walls up and started the finish work. Cabinets, drawers, fixtures, painting – each week was a new project. Our bedroom was the first area to be completely done, and I couldn't wait for the rest of the build to be finished before I unwrapped our new mattress and bedding and put it together. We laid in our freshly made bed, ignoring the construction zone still beyond it, and dreamed of the day we'd sleep here full-time. Day by day, packages containing all the items I'd had saved for months on my shopping lists arrived, and our home took shape around us until one day, quite suddenly, it was done.

You know when you have a vision, and you're not sure it will come out exactly as you see it in your head? There's a popular Netflix show we love to watch as a family called *Nailed It*, in which people try to recreate intricate baked goods within a time limit. While the contestants start with a vision in their head that matches the example, more often than not they've generally given up the vision by the end and are simply trying to get something on the plate before the timer goes off. And it's always a wry moment, when you're creating a project you saw so clearly in your head that no amount of execution seems able to pull off and you, instead, end up with a "nailed it!" moment.

The bus wasn't like that at all. Every single design aspect, the feel of the floor plan, the way it all came together – it was exactly as I saw it in my head. It was as if I'd held the dream so steady inside myself all those months, clinging to it as the only bright spot on our horizon, I'd literally willed it, exactly as I'd envisioned it, into existence. While we encountered setbacks and had to change the plan a number of times, somehow, it turned out precisely the way I'd imagined it would.

Of course, the bus today looks a lot different than our initial floor plan, as we've made adjustments based on our experiences while living and traveling in it. We traded the kids' large bunk beds for smaller twin fold out couches that allowed more living space after they expressed how much they hated the bunks, removed the washer and dryer we hardly used and replaced it with a bathtub we use all the time, and added additional storage like bookshelves and closet space into previously underutilized areas. I've been nervous at each step to make the changes – what if I hate them and they're not as good as the original design? But each time, I'm always pleasantly surprised to see it continues to exceed the vision in my head as each new addition becomes a reality.

People are always shocked when they walk inside the bus. Those who are familiar with it from our social media say, "It looks just like it does in pictures!", and those who didn't know what to expect are completely taken aback by the fact that it's "just like a real house". While there are a few amenities we do without, like that washer and dryer I mentioned or a microwave, most people simply can't believe an old school bus could possibly be such a livable little home, with all the comforts of one. For those who don't follow us on social media and aren't familiar, our tiny home on wheels boasts a living area with television, bookshelves, foldaway table, and couch. The large kitchen has a full-size RV fridge, oven/stove combo, tons of cupboard and counter space, an open-shelf pantry, and eating bar. A full bathroom sits behind it, complete with bathtub, rainfall shower, and composting toilet, and our spacious bedroom includes a Queen-sized bed, closet, and window seat. We also have a "basement", where our water and propane tanks are stored, an extensive solar system, and a roof top deck accessed through our bedroom. A wood stove keeps us warm, and the built-in wood box is large enough to hold several days of wood in. Throughout the build you'll find hidden storage and spaces that are multiuse. In other words, we used every single inch of that 250 square feet to create a tiny haven on wheels, designed just for us.

One of the first questions we're always asked is how much the whole project cost, start to finish. When embarking on bus life, one thing you learn very quickly is nothing is off limits.

Questions considered rude in normal life such as how much your home cost, how you make your money, and how much you make doing it are ones we became used to answering on a regular basis. While most people would never walk up to a home they liked, ring the doorbell, and ask to see the inside, we now expect knocks on the door most everywhere we go from people hoping to take a tour inside. Some bus lifers don't feel comfortable sharing these details, and at first it felt a little uncomfortable living our lives so much in the open, answering such personal questions. But we quickly realized people ask because they're hoping the answers mean they might be able to live a similar dream one day, and so we now comfortably share our experiences and knowledge with them. Yet another lesson bus life taught us: when we share our experiences, the good and the bad, we create space for others to do the same, reminded we are none of us, ever, completely alone in our feelings or thoughts.

In fact, I decided to include a whole chapter in this book dedicated to the frequently asked questions we receive, in case you're one of those dreamers who picked it up hoping for a blueprint to guide your own plans. While there's no one-size-fits-all approach to building a life you love, if our journey and willingness to share it means even a few people find the inspiration they need to lead a life more in alignment with who they truly are, I will bleed ink onto endless pages telling it over and over.

It wouldn't fix all the world's problems, but can you imagine how much happier a place it would be if there were more people so in love with their own lives their sole ambition simply became helping others also do more of what they love? As I absolutely am in love with my life, for the first time in the entirety of it, and with that thought in mind, my sole ambition these days is to spread that love, however possible – in this case by including a chapter with answered questions for those curious about what this lifestyle truly looks like outside the squares of social media. Sometimes love and the spreading of it simply involves living our life truthfully in the open for others to see.

We finished building the bus and took it out for the first time on my birthday, exactly one year after we pulled it into the driveway. I can't even explain how it felt pulling our newly finished home out of the gym and onto the road. I would be lying if I said there wasn't some panic. After all, every single thing I now owned and my entire family were behind the wheel in my hands. But oh, the joy of that moment. The sheer, unadulterated, childlike glee coursing through every cell of my body as the dream we'd bled and cried and worked and almost bankrupted ourselves for became a reality. All that remained was to officially move in and set off.

I don't know about you, but I'm not a fan of moving. The boxing, the driving back and forth between old and new home, the unboxing. Because I become easily bored, however, I tend to move a lot, so I've experienced the hassle of it all more times than I care to count. This time, however, part of my all-encompassing joy included the process of moving, not just from one house to another, but from one chapter to the next. I pulled Oliver up in front of our apartment and opened the door. No boxes necessary, we simply walked our remaining possessions out to the curb and moved them directly to where they'd reside in the bus. The kids spent most of their time in their bunks, organizing their clothes and belongings in their new space. Clothing, toiletries, kitchen items, décor – within a few hours, our apartment was emptied and cleaned and the house we'd built suddenly looked like a home.

A few weeks later, last of the loose ends tied up, we said our goodbyes to friends and family. Kids nestled in their bunks and brimming with excitement, essentials stocked and packed, and a map on the dash, Mike closed the front door and turned to me.

"Ready?"

Tears shining in my eyes, lump in my throat, I nodded and shifted into drive. The waves and smiles of my parents and

Evan slipped into the rearview, and the horizon opened up in front of us. Oliver was on the road.

Road Life

We drove Oliver today, for the first time ever, as our home - his maiden voyage. Stuff we hadn't thought about securing was sliding around, drawers and cupboards flew wide open, our bathroom mirror fell off the wall and at one point, while driving, our front door randomly popped open.

It was freaking glorious.

We laughed the whole way, the kids holding drawers closed, Mike holding onto the front door and me bobbing up and down in my air seat.

Because all this aside (that's what maiden voyages are for, after all), each of us was thinking the same thing - so this is what it feels like.

(May 8, 2019)

We had a rough plan for that first trip – no timelines, no set routes, just destinations we wanted to arrive at and a loose idea of how to get there. The basic itinerary was a large circle through most of the Western states, hitting national parks and points of interest along the way. We giggled to ourselves a lot that first week, all four of us somewhat stunned, after all the planning and talking and building, to be actually living it. Every ordinary moment seemed extraordinary back then – taking turns getting ready for the day in our little bathroom, making dinner and watching TV together at night. The miles rolled by as we checked firsts off our list. Filling up the water tanks, emptying the toilet, pulling up at a store to get groceries; menial tasks were suddenly precious and momentous occasions to be celebrated.

We learned almost everything we needed to know about what to expect when living in a bus that first month on the road, both beautiful and tragic. That we would find magic in unexpected places and potholes where we expected smooth roads. That life would be a careful balance, the unpredictability of a home on wheels weighed against the natural rhythm we fell into on the road. Work and school carefully juggled with driving and new places to explore. It's second nature to us now, but back then every day was an experiment in what created chaos or peace.

Driving was a huge one. We learned early on the number of miles our tires rolled over in any given day directly correlated to the overall morale inside the bus by the end of it. Long days spent pushing toward a particular destination ended with a bus full of cranky people glowering at each over a hastily prepared dinner. In the early days we had destination fever, always pushing toward the next circle on the map. We quickly adjusted our mentality and realized we needed to be more about the journey itself and how we were getting there over hopping from place to place as quickly as possible. Setting a limit on the amount of driving hours we allowed ourselves in any given day made a huge difference to the quality of our travel experience.

While our pace slowed significantly, creating this boundary showed us what we'd been missing in our haste to check locations off a list. Instead of heading out toward a fresh destination hundreds of miles away, focused only on that outcome and dealing with miles between as a hassle, we were forced to examine those roads as part of the plan. With only a few hours of driving possible in any given day, knowing we'd never make the next checkpoint within our allotted limit, we started scouting out and finding stops along the way that sometimes turned out to be better than the well-known ones on our lists. More often than not, the places we stumbled on by accident after implementing the "no more than three hours of driving" rule turned out to be our favorites. I can't count the number of times we stayed parked a day or two longer in one of those accidental spots because they were so perfect.

And it wasn't just the best way to navigate on a map we had to learn, it was how to navigate our new living situation as four people coexisting together in two hundred and fifty square feet of space. The early teenage years are tricky enough to manage in a regular home, let alone confining said teens into a small space with their parental units, the perceived cause of all wrongs. Simply getting ready in the morning, sharing a tiny bathroom, required a whole new routine be created to accommodate everyone being prepared for the day without major incident. I can tell you this – personalities take up space in a way you don't notice in a larger home. The annoying little ticks, the irritating habits, every way in which their mode of operating grates against yours are exponentially amplified in a smaller home.

I remember the first time Ellery flew into a very stereotypical teenage girl dramatic rage. At our old house, she would have flounced off into her room, likely slamming the door and blasting angsty "parents just don't understand" tunes as loud as her stereo would permit while I retired to my own room to cool off before having to confront her hormones again. Instead, her theatrics were reduced to maneuvering carefully around Mike and Aidyn as she huffed off, only managing to get ten feet away from where our argument had taken place before dropping into her bunk and angrily tearing the curtain closed. The momentum caused it to pull away from the other side, and she had to carefully straighten it back into place as the boys began to snicker. Meanwhile, as she snapped her headphones on, I removed myself as far in the opposite direction as I could to our bedroom. Mike and Aidyn retreated outside, mumbling something about crazy girls, and Ely and I glowered in our respective corners, still close enough to hear the others' angry huffs of breath.

At some point, for the sake of our respective sanities, we all seemed to come to a similar conclusion; we would need to relearn some habits to keep the peace. While it was forced out of necessity, the way we grew together living in this bus had lasting ripple effects. Try having a knockdown, drag out fight with your spouse when it has to be contained in a forty-foot vacuum. The choice between your ego and peace comes a little easier at the price of spending every waking moment with the person you've just pissed off, with no place to escape. And if that sounds terrible, I'll let you in on a little secret – it kind of is. I can think of moments I've had withering insults on the tip of my tongue, scathing retorts perfectly crafted to both wound him and fuel my own pride, swallowed instead like so much bitter medicine in the name of keeping the peace. It's galling, painful even, to force yourself to sort out a misunderstanding calmly and rationally when you are secretly and absolutely convinced you're right and they're raving.

When I think of the damage we've avoided inflicting on the other, however, by being forced to talk instead of yell and storm off, the ways in which we've been able to grow entwined instead of simply parallel, it's worth every single ounce of ego I sacrificed on the altar of bus life concessions. When you're spending every single moment with the members of your family in a tiny home, you learn very quickly to tidy up the messy parts of your personality so it requires less space. Living tiny didn't just come with downsizing our possessions. We also had to let go of some pieces of ego that didn't fit neatly into the bus. And in the same way we didn't actually need walk-in closets full of clothes and a whole drawer of Tupperware containers, we slowly found we didn't need the parts of ourselves that were easily offended or willing to sacrifice an otherwise peaceful night together in the name of anger.

Ely and I would have future fights, but with the forced closeness we learned to conduct them more fairly. When you can't run away, talking it out is really the only option left outside of the silent treatment, and trust me when I say you can only ignore someone for so long when you have to move aside to let them pass you in the hallway every ten minutes. I sometimes wonder what might have happened to my relationship with my children, had we continued to live in our old three-story house. I have nothing with which to compare it, but I can't imagine we would be as close as we are now, after spending almost every day together for the last four years. Our proximity demanded better communication, deeper understanding of the other. One thing I can say without a doubt – bus life changed our family dynamic for the better, and I'm closer to my children and Mike now than I likely would have had the chance to be in our old life.

Then there's the basics, the stuff you take for granted in a sticks and bricks home like having water for a shower or a toilet that must be emptied. You learn very quickly in bus life that anticipating issues and taking steps to prevent them is ten times more effective than simply hoping they don't arise. At first, you take things as they come. For instance, waiting until the water starts running low before looking for a spot to refill your tanks. Then you spend a day or two with only a few gallons of water left while you frantically drive around trying to find a place a to refill, and you learn to start scouting water at every stop, topping off your tanks any time there's opportunity to do so instead of waiting for them to be near empty. You adopt a checklist that takes place every time you arrive at new place or leave an old one that includes mechanical and system checks, hoping to spot problems before they actually occur.

Even then, with all the preventative measures in the world, you'll overflow your toilet or leave the bus lights on and kill your battery or have to start rationing water because you missed filling the tanks at the last stop. Every life has tradeoffs.

The difference between content and unrest in our decisions is whether they're worth the flip side.

I had kids early in my life, while my friends were going to college and living their young lives with no diapers and car seats to worry about. The tradeoff is that now, as those same peers have young kids and full-time jobs and softball schedules to keep track of, my kids are about to graduate and I will be free as a bird to, say, go turn a bus into a tiny home and spend a few years driving around the US, freelancing as I go. I'm content with this arrangement, having given up some partying and fun in my early life to essentially be able to retire early from the grind, because the flip side is the less desirable option to me. I may have had some fun by holding off on kids and marriage seventeen years ago, but to now be able to have that fun as a more self-possessed, financially responsible, and confident woman with a man like Mike beside me? Totally worth the tradeoff, in my eyes.

In the same way, bus life isn't all sunsets in beautiful locations and drinking coffee on the roof deck. Sometimes it's scrounging water and running out at midnight to pee in the woods because you forgot to empty your toilet the night before. And within that, I'm content. Magically, deliciously, absolutely content. Because I will happily empty a urine tank or deal with mechanical mishaps if only to experience even a handful of the beautiful moments we've had. The freedom to roam and disappear off-grid when the mood hits, waking up to desert sunrises and falling asleep to the rush of the ocean, spending days exploring and evenings cooking dinner and reading safe in our little home in the wild; the beautiful parts of bus life have been worth every single inconvenience we've encountered along the way.

And there are so many beautiful moments, the ones you see on social media and think "that can't possibly be real". They are, I promise. Ones I can't even adequately describe, because words just fall too far short of how incredible they are. Parked in a clearing on a hill in the high desert forest, sitting on our roof deck while the sky lit up in brilliant shades of fuchsia and gold and a herd of elk bugled in every direction around us. Taking the small winding path from our front door down through the trees to a hidden beach as the sun rose and the tide rushed out to walk among the rocky cliffs covered in thousands of brightly colored starfish and scuttling crabs the ocean left behind in its mad rush out. Alone in the vast sands of the desert, billions of stars overhead dancing to the lonesome tune of the coyotes howling in the distance. Endless cups of coffee by streams and oceans, under sunrises and sunsets, on our deck and while listening to rain on the roof.

And it isn't even totally about the far-flung and remote

destinations. Windows down and a breeze carrying our favorite road trip tunes through the bus. Potlucks in our tiny living room with other road lifers we met up with. Visiting museums and national parks with our kids and returning to our home in the parking lot to eat and watch a movie together. Driving our house right up to the grocery store to have groceries delivered. Not every moment in this bus has been beautiful. There have been tears and frustrations and setbacks and sadness. But bus life as a whole, the freedom and experiences it contains, the journey it's taken us on, absolutely is.

The Downsides of Bus Life

Someone recently asked us what the best and worst parts of bus life are. I honestly don't know if I can answer that, because the bad parts sometimes lead to the beautiful parts and vice versa. There's always a trade-off.

For instance, weathering a Montana winter in a bus with -20 temps and feet of snow is hard, but trust me when I say you've never experienced anything quite so cozy as this little bus when the wood stove is roaring and snow is drifting down outside the windows while you're drinking coffee on the couch. Finding water and parking places can be a headache, but they've also been some of our most memorable moments and funniest parts of that day's adventure.

Conversely, life on the road is a constant changing horizon that so many people wish for, but it also means being away from family and missing birthdays and breakdowns and tire blowouts and health issues in unfamiliar places. And being in far-flung remote locations and getting to drive all over seems like a huge plus, but when you consider we need Wi-Fi to work, it can be a real source of stress trying to balance travel and finding places to park while also considering our workload for the week.

I can only think of one thing that doesn't have a trade-off, and that's the sunsets. Whether we are in a parking lot or truck stop or miles and miles away from everyone, we've never seen one in this bus we didn't love. Most of the time the perks outweigh the hard stuff. Sometimes the good gets lost in a bad moment. But the sunsets are a constant.

(March 25, 2021)

Of course, now I've opened the topic of the downsides of our lifestyle, we should have a chat about them. We and others in the bus, van, and RV life communities on social media are often accused of showing only the Instagram worthy moments, highlighting the perks without disclosing the drawbacks. And it's a fair judgement, but I'd counter most people show a highlight reel of their lives. Gardening accounts rarely show the relentless weeds creeping back in, they show the fresh harvest. Interior designers depict a clean before and after, leaving the hours of work between to your imagination. Travel accounts are rife with images of far-flung destinations and perfect moments, not layovers in airports and lost luggage.

I appreciate the push for the real. In a world where photos and videos and moments can be manipulated and edited and airbrushed, it's no wonder people want to see what's raw and real. But there's an extreme side to this, where only certain moments are counted as "real". Everyone has dirty laundry in a corner somewhere, we all know this, and it's real. But for us, in this lifestyle, sitting on our bus roof watching a sunset is just as real. Just because one happens to be more beautiful doesn't make it less a part of my real life, less a reality of bus life. We take photos and videos of what we want to remember and are proud of. I don't grab my camera to document laundry all over my bed because I'm busy folding it and putting it away, but you best believe I'm going to pick it up when the sun is setting behind the mountains, hitting the bus just right in golden light, so I can remember a particular evening when the world seemed to hum with the beauty of nature and we were there to witness it.

When I'm fighting with my spouse or having a mechanical issue or the house is a mess, photographing it is generally the last thing on my mind. Do those moments occur? Of course! But I'm too busy dealing with them in real time to consider documenting it for the masses. I find where social media is concerned, most people (us included) talk openly about the struggles of the day as they happen in their stories and leave the square photos in their feeds for the memories they prefer to remember. I don't think this means people are trying to hide the bad. I think instead they like to focus on the good and show what makes the struggles worth every bit of energy they require, why the tradeoff is a fair one. They want to show you the view from the top, the height of what's possible, the absolute most beautiful version of their life for you to keep in mind as you chase your own dreams and build your own best version of life.

Going back to those tradeoffs, every life has them. I always assume people know there are inherent downsides to bus life, concessions you'll be forced to make to enjoy the more romanticized parts, just like there are for any lifestyle. There are drawbacks to living in a more traditional house, for instance, but when someone posts a picture of their beautiful home, I don't think, "Well yes, this looks nice, but how come you aren't mentioning in your 'Home Sweet Home' caption that you have a huge mortgage and can't travel as much as you'd like as a result, or that you have to mow the lawn and pay utility bills and have terrible neighbors?"

Transparency is important. When we share our bad days – unshowered and sweat pants clad for the third day in a row, covered in newborn spit up while a toddler screams, a basement flooded because the pipes broke, being laid off from a job or broken up with by the one everyone thought you'd marry or sitting on the side of the road waiting for a tow because your bus just blew a tire out and you're facing a three grand bill – we create a safe place for others to fall apart and say, yes, me too, I'm there as well and I'm so glad I'm not alone. Those moments, when we're brave enough to share them, create space where we know we aren't the only ones experiencing those uphill battles. And for the record, yes, every one of those situations is from my own personal blooper reel.

But there's this odd stigma about transparency the other way, as if people feel concerned about appearing too happy. We don't want to make anyone feel bad, after all, flaunting our success and joy. And to this I would say when we openly and honestly share our good days, our highlight reel, the places we shine, we create a different kind of space from the one above altogether. A place where dreamers are encouraged to chase their wildest ones, where hope blossoms as we begin to imagine that we, too, might be able to have and experience those beautiful moments others are offering up as living examples of possibility. Sharing your bloopers honestly is absolutely necessary to keep it real, but as any good movie will show you, you shouldn't feel bad about relegating them to the end credits after the main feature has been shown.

You'll find the less palatable aspects of bus life on our blog and social media as they arise. Our worst include blowing a tire while going seventy-five down the interstate and side swiping a telephone pole. As a matter of fact, a quick dig into the nomadic community at large will turn up numerous blog and social media posts talking downsides. Ask any road lifer if there are drawbacks, and they will unabashedly rattle off a whole list of what they've personally experienced for you.

And that's the other aspect to consider. Even within the same lifestyle, you'll have vastly different experiences. We've known people in the community who had nothing but troubles from day one – mechanical issues, breakdowns, tire blowouts, rust and moisture problems, parking in places they were chased away from, family that didn't agree with their choices, the works. If you asked them what bus life looks like, it would be a dramatically different answer from my own, which has been overwhelmingly positive.

All that said, there are downsides. And what is an acceptable tradeoff for a personality like mine could be a dealbreaker for another. I would be absolutely remiss if I didn't take this opportunity to talk about them for the sake of the aforementioned dreamers reading this book and pondering bus life for themselves. You want to drink coffee on your roof deck while the sun rises over a jaw droppingly beautiful vista and experience a feeling of freedom and joy so absolute you'll literally have moments tears course down your cheeks? Prepare to hear the tradeoffs friends.

Let's start with maintenance. All homes come with at least a little bit, unless perhaps you're renting or have services employed. Mowing the lawn, shoveling snow, cleaning, repairing appliances, dealing with those rare occurrences like a leaking roof or badly settled foundation; owning a home means taking care of it. And while you won't have a lawn to mow every weekend in summer or a walk to shovel every day in winter, you will be signing on for a list of maintenance work unique to life on the road.

You live in a home with wheels and an engine, which come with their own needs. And it isn't just your run of the mill car-style maintenance, you're going to need to bone up on air brakes, intricate electrical systems, and the nuances of one exceptionally large diesel engine. Prepare to constantly learn new information related to caring for systems you were blissfully unaware of before you drove an old school bus home. And if something happens to break down mechanically? Your whole home will be going to the repair shop. If it's a quick fix, like a tire or oil change, no biggie, you'll be home again before you know it. If it's a major repair, however? You are suddenly homeless until yours comes out of the shop and will need to find a nearby hotel or stay with friends and family until the issue is resolved.

Then there's the myriad of daily maintenance, the chores that come along with having a home not attached to the grid. If you choose an RV-style toilet with a black tank, get used to finding places to stop and drag out a hose to pump the contents out. A composting toilet saves you that particular trouble, but you'll still need to empty the contents every few weeks and deal with the much more frequent dumping of a urine tank. Almost every road lifer we know has some kind of toilet-related horror story with a lesson attached. And it doesn't stop at your bathroom. I will never again take for granted the magic of flipping a switch and having a light turn on, turning on the tap to fill a bath with hot water, or preheating an oven with the turn of a knob.

There is constant checking and filling to make sure you can enjoy these luxuries while on the road. Finding potable water to fill your tanks can be difficult, especially in certain parts of the country. We actually ended up installing a filtration system for our drinking water so we wouldn't have to worry in the event we had to scrounge and be less choosy about where we were filling up. Sometimes it's easy to find RV-friendly hookups with fresh, clean water. Other times you'll look all day, be turned down at multiple places even when you're offering to pay, and finally settle for a garden hose behind a friendly tire shop. Propane is easier, as the tanks are smaller and almost any gas station will have it, but I will never forget the day our stove turned off right in the middle of making dinner and we discovered we'd forgotten to fill the backup tank.

Your solar system will also need maintenance. You'll quickly learn even a small amount of dirt on your panels can cause their efficiency to be drastically reduced, meaning crawling up on the roof to remove whatever has dared block those precious rays of sun that translate to the power you'll want later when you try to Netflix and chill for the night. Driving through dusty terrain? Wipe them off. It rained? Wipe them off. Snow? Shove it all off. It's not a constant issue like emptying your urine tank, but the chore is frequent enough to warrant mention. The rest of the system will need troubleshooting from time to time as well, as lights you've never noticed on your charge controller suddenly start blinking dire warnings or your inverter begins an ominous beeping sound while you're lying in bed one night enjoying a movie. When we traveled through the deserts of the Southwest in January, we had to make sure we were driving every few days to let the alternator give our house batteries an extra charge since the sun wasn't passing directly overhead and didn't fully charge us up every day.

Then there's the heating and cooling issue. Your home is a giant metal tube on wheels, and no matter how well insulated, you will struggle to maintain a steady temperature and humidity in your living space in extreme temperatures. Many bus lifers deal with condensation and mold issues in areas with higher humidity. Some chase the sunshine and midrange temperatures, choosing to follow good weather through the year. By avoiding the hottest places during the summer and staying far south during the winter, they work to ensure they'll never have to deal with temperatures and weather at extremes. For others who are more stationary for periods of time, you're looking at finding cooling and heating solutions that are compatible with the energy you have available. People often ask us why we chose a wood stove for our heating needs instead of installing an electric or gas-fired heating unit, and the answer is it's cheap and provides dry heat, a plus in a condensation prone home. Electric appliances with a heating unit would require a much larger solar system than we have to run, propane heaters give off condensation, and a diesel heater would require yet another tank to remember to fill. We collect wood through the course of the year mostly for free, meaning our home stays warm through a Montana winter on the cheap. Plus, you just can't beat that crackling sound of burning wood as you watch the snow fall outside your windows.

The costs need to be considered. While you won't be paying for rent or a mortgage, you will be paying for fuel. Obviously the more you choose to drive, the higher your fuel costs will be. On the flip side, if you decide to park and chill for a while, you might still be paying. We park almost exclusively on public and family land, where it's free, but others pay to park long term at RV parks and campsites. I remember in

Oregon we paid $30 a night for an RV park because that stretch of coast had no parking signs everywhere. Oil changes, new tires, repair fees – your home on wheels comes with all kinds of new considerations you'll have to budget for.

Space is at a premium when your home is less than two hundred and fifty square feet. When I lived in a larger home, I remember thinking nothing of seeing something I liked at a local store and bringing it home with me. Now there's a process that takes place each and every time. Will I actually use this? Where will it live when I'm not using it? Is it worth the space it takes up? Do I already have something similar I could use instead? While I would actually list this as a perk, in that it's forced me into conscious consumerism instead of mindlessly buying junk I don't need, the lack of space is a definite downside for some people. Every inch of it counts, and while you'll learn how to make the most of each precious nook and cranny, you'll also likely have to forgo some items because there's simply not room. Similarly, when you're designing your layout, you might be forced to prioritize what's more important and leave certain details out in lieu of what you've deemed more essential to life on the road.

That life on the road also means your home is basically in an earthquake zone. On our first trip out, I made a cake to celebrate, and, still new to bus life, we absentmindedly left the plate sitting on the counter when we took off again. An hour later we took a turn, and with an earsplitting crash the remaining cake tumbled to the floor, glass and chocolate flying in every direction. Everything that isn't nailed down is at risk of moving, and even with precautions in place you'll have accidents, like when we didn't push the fridge closed well enough to make the lock latch and it flew open while driving. Museum wax, command strips, cupboard locks, and bungee nets help hold possessions in place, but no matter how well you built your home or secured your belongings, you will inevitably be making repairs and cleaning up messes from time to time as the constant jostling over bumpy roads causes things to shake loose.

Parking and driving are further considerations. Short buses and vans can go just about anywhere and park discreetly in parking lots, but if you want the space a forty-foot bus likes ours offers you'll have no such luck. Routes must be vetted ahead of time. A low overpass, narrow street, or tiny parking lot can turn into a road blocking and stress inducing situation. You'll sometimes have to choose between parking the bus and finding other transportation in order to experience certain attractions or skipping them altogether. You'll get knocks on your door at night because the people living up the hill don't appreciate you've parked within their view and your home is considered an eyesore to them. You'll pull into gas stations to discover they don't have a second exit and be required to execute a 20-point turnaround between the pumps to get back onto the road.

We wanted to visit Sedona while in the Southwest. For those who aren't familiar, the road there involves a stretch of switchbacks through the mountains. I can tell you now, they were not considering a vehicle like our Oliver when building that beautiful but curvy portion of highway. However, we navigated through without incident, pulling over where the shoulder allowed to let others pass us as we were forced to drive more slowly through the hairpin turns. Once in Sedona, we discovered the main road was studded with roundabouts. And even that wasn't a deal breaker – while maneuvering a forty-foot straight line of a vehicle with no turning point through a tight circle isn't fun, it's doable if you're paying attention and going slow. The real problem came when Siri, who was navigating us to the parking lot we planned to park in, told us to take the first right off the next roundabout. The moment the bus exited the main road, I knew we'd made a mistake. Because ahead of us wasn't an actual road, but a driveway our navigation hadn't accounted for.

Immediately in front of us, the drive masquerading as the first turn went steeply uphill and turned sharply right in a complete one-eighty turn. Short of reversing into the oncoming traffic of the roundabout, however, we had no choice but to gun it up the narrow lane. The stunned driver of the Mercedes convertible coming round the turn suddenly found himself nose to nose with a very out of place, large white school bus and promptly reversed course back up the hill to allow us into the turn. The traffic behind us stalled as I swung wide to fit through the curve, barely breathing while trying to both delicately fit the bus around a corner and keep enough speed to get us up the incredibly steep incline. The few seconds it took to make that godforsaken turn stretched into an eternity; Mike chanted a litany of encouragement behind me while I shrieked a string of swear words, the people above and below us stopped in traffic to watch the circus unfolding, and then finally, we made it through the turn and continued up the hill. It dead-ended into the parking lot of a ritzy hotel, the guests of which stared with open mouths as our home crept carefully through to the next street where we could regain the main road and take the actual right turn Siri had intended us to take.

But even in that moment, as I recall this story, I don't immediately think of the way my gut sank down to the pedals as our predicament dawned on me, or how I almost bawled when we parked a few moments later out of sheer relief not to be behind the wheel anymore.

You see, right after that happened, we pulled safely (if a little shaken) into the parking lot we'd preplanned parking in. As I pulled out my phone to turn off navigation, I noticed a new DM had just popped in from a local business, Sedona Water Works. Turns out, the owners had followed us the last part of the way into town and witnessed our wrong turn. From their perspective, our little jaunt uphill and tight turn looked impressive rather than terrifying, and they wanted to let us know they thought our rig was super cool. They also offered us a free fill up on water at their store. We did actually need water, but still shaken, I wasn't quite ready to try to trek back through the roundabouts of town. I started to turn them down, only to realize the parking lot in which we now sat happened to be theirs. We ended up spending the entire afternoon in that lot chatting with them, giving tours to the employees and enjoying one through their store. In a further moment of Sedona kismet, we discovered they also happened to be friends with the skoolie family we were on our way to meet when we left.

That lot also bordered a grocery store and laundry mat, and as we needed both we decided to pop our laundry in and stock up on food before heading out into the wild again. A yellow short bus was parked on the side road, and as we stuffed our dirty clothes into the washer, we discovered the store's owner had just purchased it with the intention of turning it into a skoolie and passed some time in conversation with him. And the grocery store was chock full of vegan goodies, including an amazing raisin bagel with tofu cream cheese I still dream about. The moral of the story, and this chapter, is this.

There are ugly moments in bus life. There are downsides and drawbacks and tradeoffs and sacrifices and harrowing, gut-wrenching moments. But right now, as I sit here writing this, none of them matter. If you asked me whether I would make the same choices, do this life over again, my answer would be a resounding and unqualified yes.

Because every single part of it – every scary moment, every headache, every bit of maintenance, every bump in the road, every sacrifice we made; for even a fraction of the moments we've been able to enjoy between, I would do it all over again. The biggest downside, simply put, is that someday it will end and these moments, even the hard ones, will only be memories. Because the reality of bus life, the rawest truth possible, is that even at its ugliest, it's still the most beautiful version of life I've ever known.

Where the Mountains Meet the Ocean

We were lucky enough to witness an Oregon coast sunset that rivaled any we'd ever seen (outside of Rome, you know I'm partial to Rome's sunsets), right outside our bedroom window where we parked for the night. I'm such a sucker for a good sunset.

(July 19, 2019)

The ocean waves are crashing against the cliffs, rushing in to cover the rocky outcroppings where hours before, we'd clambered between the tidal pools formed at low tide. The bus is perched above the roiling water, the salty breeze blowing gently through the windows as we sit on our couch drinking coffee and revisiting the day's excursions. Sand dollars and shells dry in a bowl on the counter, and in the back, I can hear the movie the kids have chosen to watch along with their muted conversation.

He breaks through my reverie. "Thank you," he says.

I smile, confused. "For what?"

"For this," he replies. "This life. I was just thinking about all the places we've lived. Your van, that small, shitty apartment, my mom's, Evan's, our old house, the last apartment. This is the best one, and I never would have done it without you. I'm cherishing every moment. Like this one, drinking coffee and listening to the ocean. Thank you, for convincing me we could do this. It's a gift."

This is Oregon, where the mountains meet the rolling waves of the Pacific. White sand beaches filled with sand dollars and rusty shipwrecks, cliffsides teaming with seals and gulls, where the waves crash against the stone to carve deep caves, mellow inlets of tidal pools that quickly fill when the surf rushes back to meet the land. We eat cherries we pick at roadside orchards along the way and lick melting ice cream from our fingers as we walk along boardwalks. Fog shrouds the dense green forests in the morning, creating an otherworldly mood as my toes sink into the cold sand and I watch the crabs scuttle back toward the retreating waves. The sun eventually breaks over the mountain and through the clouds, sending the mist shrinking back and flooding the beach below in golden light.

When we were building the bus, we often talked about where we'd explore, and this stretch of coastal highway was always near the top of my list. It was the last place I'd seen my family happy together before my dad died, and the magical memories I carried from that time propelled it to near legendary status in my mind. You know the ones I mean, those lasting recollections of a place or movie or song or event that leave such an impression we create shrines to them in the deep recesses of our minds? They're the places you tell your friends and family about in terms like "indescribable", the movies you insist on making people sit through so they can finally understand how good it is, the events you still talk about years later.

It's hard to live up to that kind of hype. In fact, more often than not when I revisit these old memories to share them with others and let them in on the magic, I usually find whatever spell I was under at the time has lifted, the alchemy gone. Those moments each have a unique creationary blend of components hard to reproduce, and when I try to repeat an experience, my conjuring to replicate it mostly falls short of the original. Every so often, however, one of these fabled experiences truly does come through again in living color instead of a pale imitation. Oregon was one of these.

In fact, we loved it so much, we actually considered buying land there. While we drove, we turned down promising little lanes that meandered into the woods where a "For Sale" sign showed through the wild tangle by the road. We read the fliers taped in real estate office windows as we strolled down the streets of little coastal towns. At the end of the day, however, we'd return to our little home on wheels and realize there was still a lot of road our tires hadn't rolled over yet, and we weren't ready to consider having even shallow roots yet.

It wasn't all pink sunsets over the rolling waves and exploring the wild, emerald-green forests, however. Oregon was also where we were in our first and only accident, the only place we ever truly struggled to find parking, and the place we ran into our first big mechanical issue. But to this day, it remains in my memory bank hall of fame not once, but twice, as one of the most beautiful places I've ever had the privilege of seeing.

It was on the narrow streets of Canon Beach Oliver received his battle scar. Right hand turns in a bus are tricky, trying to get your front half out far enough for the back half to clear the turn while simultaneously ensuring you aren't swinging the front out into oncoming traffic from the other lane. When we arrived, we navigated carefully and slowly into a parking lot with long RV spots and spent the day enjoying the small shops along the beach and the tidal pools along the massive conical rocks jutting out from the seabed at low tide. When we went to leave, however, disaster struck for the first time in bus life.

People are always shocked or bemused when they learn I'm Oliver's main driver. I suppose they just expect to see Mike behind the wheel of such a large vehicle. The semi drivers we pass on the interstates are always my favorite, as they whip around for a second glance and sometimes honk or wave or give me a thumbs up when they notice the little woman behind the wheel. Growing up in a rural community meant I was exposed to driving plenty of farm vehicles from the time I was young, so I've always felt comfortable in the driver's seat of the bus. It was somewhat more of a learning curve for Mike, but by this point he was fairly comfortable. It was this incident at Cannon Beach, however, that caused him to excuse himself almost entirely from driving duty.

We loaded back into the bus, and Mike decided to take the wheel. Up to that point, we traded off driving. I did the majority of it, as he worked while I drove, but every so often he'd ask if he could drive and take over at the helm so I could relax on the couch. Our driving styles were very different. I prefer to take my time. While I try to be conscious of the other drivers on the road, I'm also not afraid to go slow and hold up traffic a bit if it's necessary. After all, my entire home and the people I love are behind me when I drive, and I won't risk their safety because someone else is in a rush to turn. There's a careful balance between being a considerate road mate to the travelers around me and being slow and mindful in certain situations. Normally, people are good natured about waiting a moment or going a little slower for short time.

But Mike is a person who considers everyone else's feelings to a fault, and it shows when he drives. He's so concerned with inconveniencing or holding people up he tries to rush, and it was this tick of his that caused him to hurry the right turn out of the parking lot and cut it too close. The bus mounted the curb and, with a shrieking screech of metal, sideswiped the massive wood telephone pole on the corner. There was a high-pitched keening as the bus scraped along the pole, a split-second pause as the tire caught the wood, and then with a massive shudder the bus heaved free and jounced off the curb. We had to go a few blocks down to find a shoulder to pull off on as we all stared wide-eyed at each other, afraid to get out and survey the damage after the apocalyptic sounds we'd just heard.

Thankfully, it wasn't that bad. The stained wood had left dark streaks down the metal side, and the tire showed similar battle scars, but neither was in any other way disfigured. The metal didn't have even the smallest dent. Mike jogged back to check out and deal with whatever damages we'd caused to the pole and came loping back five minutes later to report there was no evidence a large school bus had only moments before tried to bring it down. There weren't even tire marks on the curb. Somehow, despite the way it'd sounded from inside the bus, the actual event had been fairly unremarkable.

From that moment on, however, Mike decided he no longer cared to drive much. As my very type A personality had struggled to enjoy the trip from the passenger seat, I was totally okay with this development. I've come to realize over time, however, that in the way he tends to, he used that moment as an excuse to give me what I secretly wanted without hurting my feelings. Rather than simply saying, "Listen, you're a terrible backseat driver and I think you should just do all the driving to save us both from your anxiety", he used that minor accident as a way to thoughtfully arrange our driving situation in a way I wouldn't feel bad about later. In a pinch, Mike is fully capable of maneuvering the bus and getting us from point A to point B. But for the most part, the driver's seat is now mine, and it's a point of pride for both of us. I sometimes overhear him talking to friends or family, bragging about the tight spots I've navigated us in and out of.

"I took a look at it and said, 'Nah, there's no way we're getting in there', but Tawny just got out and looked around, kicked a rock out of the way, and said, 'I can do it'. And lo and behold, somehow, the next thing I know, she's made this perfect little turn and wiggled her way into the spot." His frequent joke is I'm the bus driver that would have made all the kids happy to go to school.

And I do love driving Oliver. The beeping as I turn the key. The rumble of that big diesel engine firing up behind me. He always seems to leap out of his spot when we take off, as if as eager to be on the way again as we are. I often pat the dash as I drive in an encouraging sort of way, talking to him about what a good boy he is as if he were a living trusty steed instead of a giant mechanical one. I reassure him as we pull up long hills, telling him I'm so proud of him and that he's doing so well. I thank him as I turn off the ignition for transporting us to yet another location safe and sound. I promise him a wash when we get back to home base, and from time to time, you'll even see the curly-haired driver hop down the stairs and throw her arms around the behemoth's metal nose in a grateful gesture.

Of course, every so often my mechanical friend has an issue that requires immediate attention. We've been incredibly lucky to escape any major malfunctions. Waiting for a mechanically sound bus that had been well-cared for and always doing routine maintenance have definitely paid off and helped. As I mentioned, however, it wasn't just our first accident we encountered while in Oregon; we also had to address our first big mechanical issue. We'd just parked for the night in a Wal-

Mart lot, where we planned to restock on groceries, ready to head back out into the wild the next day. I mentioned the brakes felt a little sluggish, so Mike opened the hatch above to door to release the humidity out of the air system for me, a simple matter of twisting a plastic screw to allow it to escape before retightening it. As he turned it, however, a classic "Miking" moment happened, and the small plastic stopper broke in his hands. With a rush, all the air in our tanks whooshed out. In those few seconds, our bus went from totally road worthy to undriveable, as without sufficient pressure in the tanks, the bus won't even turn on.

Why such an important piece of the system was made of plastic I'll never know, but we simply felt grateful to be parked in front of a store instead of somewhere more remote. We figured we'd find a matching screw in the hardware section to replace the plastic one and carried on with our plan of restocking. Sure enough, we found a similarly sized screw that looked like it would do the job. As Mike put away groceries, I set to work installing the new piece, only to find the original screw was threaded backwards. Another trip into the hardware section yielded more possibilities, but ultimately, nothing we found worked. We finally gave up and went to bed for the night, deciding fresh eyes in the morning light would be better.

While Mike made breakfast from our newly stocked pantry

with the kids the next morning, I employed every ounce of MacGyvering I possessed to find a solution. A combination of a screw that didn't quite fit, plumber's putty, duct tape, and super glue finally resulted in a seal. We all held our breaths as I turned the key and cheered as the bus roared back to life and the tanks slowly refilled. Within a few minutes, Oliver was back to himself, carrying us further down the coast.

Mishaps like those were almost always the basis for another round of learning. Not only did we discover quite a lot about our air system, we also took steps shortly down the road to ensure we shouldn't have future problems with it and added a few pieces of equipment and tools to the box we carry so we would be better equipped to fix similar problems that might arise. Plus, we chalked another lesson in bus life up; even when you're not on an active adventure, bus life is one big one in and of itself, sometimes even in a Wal-Mart parking lot.

During that same week we stayed at an RV park for the first time, unable to find any of the free parking spots on public lands we usually stick to. The Oregon coast, to deal with the huge influx of RV traffic the summer months brings, has no parking signs posted everywhere. The usual one-night pull-offs you can count on in other states like rest stops, large shoulder pullouts, and recreation areas were carefully monitored to ensure compliance with the signage. Finally, after a long day of driving and no available parking in sight, we pulled into an RV park. While the park was completely booked, upon learning we didn't need hookups they allowed us to pay a smaller fee of thirty dollars to park in their lot for the night. In the sea of Class A motorhomes and pull-behinds, Oliver definitely stuck out from the crowd.

While parking in more remote, off-grid locations will always be our favorite, we ended up staying at that park for two days. Having the chance to fill up our tanks, do laundry, and explore the nearby town without having to drive the bus everywhere between was a different kind of magic from one lived entirely on the road. All we'd wanted to do for years was travel nonstop, so imagine our surprise to find it felt nice to just sit still. It would be months later we'd park the bus again for an extended period of time somewhere, but this first time we took a little break from the road and stayed still for a few days gave us a little peek into what our future would look like.

A Too Small Box

Last night, we were lying in bed, talking about the New Year and future plans and the crazy ride this last one has been. We talked about leaving in a few days to head down to Skooliepalooza and the desert, what needed to get done before we head away from Montana. And the more we talked, the more we realized neither of us actually wanted to leave right now.

The kids are happy. We have family going through a rough patch that need us around. And most of all, we are settled right now - content, for once, to simply stay put. It just doesn't feel like the right time to leave this place.

"But you built this home to roll, why live in a bus if you aren't going to move whenever you feel like it?"

And that was the aha moment friends. Because we don't feel like it. Not at all. Right now we are enjoying a moment of peace and happiness and time spent with family tucked away for the winter. Bus life means you get a choice to move whenever you feel like it, a different view out your window every day if you choose.

It also means you get a choice when NOT to move, when to hibernate and be still. My resolution last year was to listen to my intuition and trust myself to know the truth. Our hearts tell us we aren't meant to head South right now, as much as I want to see those desert sunsets. We will. But not this month.

This month, we stay right here, cuddled up under electric blankets with steaming mugs of fresh coffee - hearts and gas tank full.

(December 19, 2019)

As the year wound down, we were making plans to travel South to Arizona to participate in our first Skooliepalooza. As the name implies, it's an annual meeting of road lifers held every year where hundreds of skoolies from all around the country converge in the desert to celebrate bus life. There are potlucks, entertainment in the evenings, workshops during the day, and the chance to talk to fellow bus, RV, and van lifers about the joys and trials of the road. We'd been finishing up the build the year before, so this was our first chance to go and participate as actual bus lifers.

After traveling around the Western United States for a few months, we'd journeyed to Bali, where we'd stayed for a month while the bus waited at home for us. I will backtrack to talk about our time on the Island of the Gods, but for now, after a whirlwind of bus and international travel, we'd returned to spend the holidays with family and for the first time since that brief Oregon detour, simply remained in one place for an extended period of time. Evan had invited us to park in his backyard so we could be close to the kids, and it had been a peaceful few weeks as we celebrated Thanksgiving and Christmas with our loved ones while still enjoying our little home on wheels. It was also our first winter in the bus, and I will never forget how cozy and magical it all seemed, as the snow drifted down outside our windows and our little wood stove crackled away inside.

While preparing to head South, however, an uncomfortable little lump of misgivings had settled into my gut. "Do you really want to be back on the road right now?" it asked.

I quickly dismissed the doubts as some misplaced fears over jumping into travel again, not pausing to think how very out of place such fears would be for a personality like mine. But every day, the little voice echoed a little louder in the corners of my mind, until I started arguing with it, trying desperately to convince it that heading out again was wanted and necessary. We'd already fielded some comments from friends, after all, during this pause in traveling. "Why build a bus if you're just going to stay in one place?" they asked.

Finally, with only weeks until we were to leave, I brought the subject up one night with Mike.

"I know this sounds strange, but I keep having this feeling like we're not supposed to go right now. Isn't that odd?" I suddenly blurted out as we lounged in bed watching a movie.

He sat up and paused the movie, and I was in no way

prepared when he swiveled on the bed to face me and say, "You know, I've been feeling the exact same thing. I didn't know how to tell you, because we've been talking about going to this for months. But it's like the time just isn't right."

It took us awhile to reason through our options and decide how we felt. After all, there was a plan in place. Did we really want to upset it and create a new one, especially one that meant staying stationary after all our work to create a home that didn't have to be?

"I don't know Mike. I mean, our social media is all about our travels. We built a home on wheels so we could. Isn't the whole point of bus life traveling whenever you want to?"

He looked at me evenly. "But isn't what we're saying right now, is that we *don't* want to?"

The question completely stopped whatever I'd been about to say. Because he was right. Yes, our home *could* travel whenever we desired, but what if that wasn't our current desire? What if our present joy was relaxing into a season of rest after two years of non-stop building and travel? Were we obligated to disrupt that peace simply because it was expected of us, both from others and our own perceptions?

And suddenly, I realized I'd put myself back into a box, one where I felt ashamed if I wasn't traveling nonstop. After all the time and effort spent breaking out of the American Dream box so we could be free, here we were feeling trapped again, this time by the idea that constant travel wasn't just the ideal, but a must for our life.

Those metaphorical boxes are funny, aren't they? Some boxes we stay in and they expand with us; I became a mother seventeen years ago and I will forever after remain a mom, a box that grows and changes as my children age. Other boxes we alter slightly to fit us as time passes, reinforcing the edges a bit as we add more to them. But many we simply outgrow. People, hobbies, places, careers, old versions of ourselves we wear like baggy clothing that no longer fits exactly right.

At one time, I couldn't have imagined a life outside of fitness and the gym we owned. Helping people become better renditions of themselves emotionally and physically, the drive and goal-oriented lifestyle, lifting heavy weights – I ate, breathed, and lived fitness for almost a decade. And then, as you've read, I started to outgrow the lifestyle little by little. Smashing through my own personal records to set new ones lost its appeal. Instead of jumping into bed at night satisfied with a day of helping people, I started falling into it drained and exhausted from the emotional demands. The long days I used to glory in took a toll on my physical health, while the constant striving to be better, better, better became a detriment to my emotional and mental wellbeing. One day, the box that used to fit me so well had instead become a tiny prison cell, one I strained against until we broke free into bus life and travel.

And when we started that life, the traveling one we'd dreamed about and built with our own two hands, I would have laughed in your face if you'd told me that constant travel would become another too small box I'd feel similarly about someday. Fortunately this prison was more metaphorical than physical, one of the boxes I needed only alter a bit rather than completely escape from, but it was still an idea I found myself trapped by, straining against. For the person who spends all day at a nine to five (or in our case, four am to seven pm), the idea of traveling non-stop is hashtag living the dream. But when it becomes an obligation, a duty to constantly have a new horizon in front of you because that's what's now expected, I will tell you it can become just as tedious as being tied to a desk all day.

The next day, I posted to tell our followers and friends expecting us at Skooliepalooza we'd decided not to travel as we'd been planning to. That we'd realized just because our home had wheels didn't mean we were obligated to keep them rolling. That we were content to just stay still for a bit, listening to our intuition the time wasn't right. And that we'd just realized the true freedom of bus life was in having options. We didn't have to always be roaming. Sometimes, when it felt right, we could stay rooted instead. While I do and will likely always love and want to travel, I learned at that moment it wasn't necessary to my happiness. The box that held my idea of what our life needed to look like in order to hold meaning and joy expanded to hold this new concept of the best of both worlds, and we've lived that way since, sometimes rambling like tumbleweeds on a windy day, blown wherever the mood takes us, sometimes settling into a place for days or weeks or months at a time to savor the luxuries of stillness.

I also started consciously making sure I wasn't putting myself into any more boxes, even well-intentioned ones. Every belief we have, every title we hold, they're all boxes we start to build around ourselves. And I've now decided we're shoved into enough boxes based on others' perceptions of us without adding more of our own to the mix. People will constantly try to put you into a box for their own comfort. If they can fit you neatly into a category in their mind, you make sense to them. Your political and religious choices, your job and salary, your lifestyle choices – in short order, you can be summed up and tidily boxed into their mental cabinet in a way you can be easily understood and just as easily dismissed if it's more comfortable. "Oh, you're a (insert box name here)? Well in that event, your opinions and choices don't matter to me, because that's a box I don't personally care for."

It's the ones who don't fit tidily into the boxes who really gum up the works. Take us, for instance. We're vegan hippies who live in a bus. Easily filed away, just a couple of liberal hipsters drinking French-pressed coffee and gentrifying homelessness while they enjoy their trustafarian status. These are actual comments taken from our social platforms, the boxes people want to file us away in. Vegan. Hippies. Liberals. Trust fund babies. Hipsters. But scratch beyond the surface of a viral video and you quickly learn we're working-class people who grew up poor and fought and worked for every single part of the life we now enjoy. That we're also gun-toting free-thinkers who don't trust big government. The truth is we don't really belong in a singular box. I'm neither conservative nor liberal. I live small but enjoy luxury. I believe everyone deserves kindness and needs a helping hand from time to time, but I was also taught you need to pull yourself up by the bootstraps and make things happen in your own life. That we are all utterly deserving and simultaneously not owed anything.

But it's not just me, is it? Hardly anyone fits tidily into a singular box. We are all of us walking contradictions. Few people lead lives entirely black and white, cut and dried. Most of us dwell firmly in the gray, a little of this and a little of that. We sometimes aren't entirely understood by the people around us. And that's totally okay. Another of bus life's little lessons — your life doesn't have to make sense to anyone else. You are under absolutely no obligation to fit inside a box to make other people more comfortable in theirs. Sometimes, when I'm reading through the comments section of our social media, I have to repeat this truth, reminding myself I owe no explanation for my life and why I'm happy in it. I can leave them to their misconceptions and move on; those boxes and matching filing system they're trying to put me in are only applicable in their own minds after all, not mine. And when it comes to boxes pertaining to misconceptions about bus life, that's a whole other chapter. The next one, actually.

Suffice it to say, after all this talk of boxes, I'm happy not to push myself into them anymore. I'm simply grateful to live a life I love, one that makes sense to me if no one else. And one I don't need a vacation from. It used to feel like there were two distinct versions of me, two different women sharing this person named Tawny. As a Gemini, duality is definitely a theme in my life – it's been the running joke of my family that I have multiple personalities, that being married to me is a grand adventure because you're never quite sure which woman is driving that particular day. Are you married to calm, rational, let's bake bread Tawny or crazy, dance naked under the moon Tawny today? In this particular instance, we can call these two different women, the two different versions, vacation Tawny and normal life Tawny. Vacation Tawny was the one smiling in those travel photos for two weeks a year, relishing every moment, climbing mountains and laying poolside with a coconut in hand. Real life Tawny mostly just looked forward to the moments she could become vacation Tawny as she dealt with the daily grind and planning the next adventure. It truly felt like two different people, neither better nor worse, but one definitely happier than the other.

One of the most noticeable changes bus life brought to me as an individual was in helping me reconcile those two very different women into one. Don't get it twisted; the nature of my twin sign will probably always be noticeable in my mercurial personality. But the longer I've lived in this bus, the more I've observed the melding of those two different versions of myself into a singular one. In building a life I love, that only requires I be the truest version of myself, there's no need to trade between the woman who allows herself to let go and feel alive in stolen moments away from her "real life" and the one who stays buttoned up to get shit done in the meantime.

Instead, I might say there's two modes now, born that day we realized we didn't need to stick to any strict definition of what bus life was supposed to look like and could create our own. Let's call them travel mode and rooted mode. I slip easily between the two. In travel mode I'm an explorer, a well of infinite energy with one eye always on the next horizon. My rooted mode is content to simply exist at our home base with a cup of coffee in my hand, enjoying the peace of this life we've built. The holes where my little roots reside are well-formed, so that when I come back to our home base and unfurl them, they sink straight and true back into place, ready to hold me safe and sound while we rest. But they're also shallow; I slip out of them at a moment's notice when the road sings its siren song to me and my feet begin itching to adventure again. Neither mode is better than the other, but neither is happier either. Their joy is simply different.

On the road or not, secluded in the woods with Mike or sitting down to dinner with family, boarding a plane to another country or working in my garden, I'm whole and I'm happy. And the only box I now currently reside in is this metal one on four wheels that changed my life and how I live it.

Misconceptions About Bus Life

Wanna hear something funny?

We've learned that if we say, "We sold everything and built a tiny home on wheels to travel more", people are like, oh sweet, that's awesome! If we say, "We live in a school bus", we sometimes instead get a distinct look that says we are dirty hippies.

For instance, when Tiny Home Tours did a YouTube tour, we got an overwhelming positive response - because it was a targeted audience that enjoys stories about alternative housing. When The Daily Mail picked up the same story and aired it to the general public instead, the comments were largely about how we were dirty hippies living in a glorified trailer and likely living off the government.

Perception is a funny thing. Someone cuts you off in traffic and you get boiling mad - because what a jerk move. What you don't know is that person's mother just died and it's all they can do to function, let alone drive well. And suddenly, it's totally understandable and you're not mad.

One of my continuing goals for myself is to constantly look outside my own perception, especially in situations where I don't understand something - like why someone would want to live in a school bus. To answer that question, by the way - because we are almost completely debt free, have no huge monthly mortgage and utility bills to pay, get to change our front yard whenever the mood hits, and spend all day, every day, with our kiddos.

And for that, I'm okay being a dirty hippie.

(December 12, 2019)

This is an interesting topic to broach, the misconceptions surrounding nomadic life. Walking a line between explaining the subject matter in a helpful way, allowing people to remove themselves from their own perceptions to have a view into ours and clear up some false ideas, while simultaneously not getting snarky or defensive (neither overly conducive to productive or meaningful conversations) is a delicate balance. When someone is making rash generalizations and assumptions about your lifestyle that aren't true, it's sometimes hard not to respond in kind and fire back in a similar tone.

But it helps to remember misconceptions are based, by definition, on faulty logic or ignorance of the topic. So right now, I'd like to take a moment to clear away some of those false deductions and assumptions about nomadic life. I want to set the record straight both for those people holding this book with a dream of bus life in their own hearts, who might be letting uninformed narratives cause them to hesitate, and also for my fellow brave and creative and amazing nomad friends who are measured wrongly by them.

When I started this chapter, I already had a list of misconceptions we were used to hearing from our social media. But I took it one step further and asked our followers about their perceptions regarding bus life. From those living it, I asked about assumptions they'd had prior to bus life versus what they'd found to be true in real life. For the rest, I asked what it appeared to be from the outside looking in. And I received so many responses I wasn't expecting, both positive and negative. Because misconceptions aren't always just negative – sometimes assumptions are overly optimistic, and as we've discussed, bus life has downsides. In addition, as fate would have it, the week I was writing this particular section our social media was absolutely bombarded with nonstop assumptions in the comments section, so I come to this chapter armed with all kinds of misconceptions about our lifestyle.

The topic of money is a huge one. How we make it, how much it cost to build a bus, the expenses of living on the road – the financial aspects of nomadic life are a big question mark in people's minds. As a matter of fact, questions surrounding money are always our most frequent. How do we make money? How much did it cost to build the bus? How much is gas and parking? What are the other expenses of bus life? We have written numerous blog articles on the subject, answered what must be thousands of comments and DMs and emails, made posts and videos, and even created a downloadable PDF for our website with every single step we took to get to this point financially. It's a hot topic of discussion around our little corner of the web.

When it comes to misconceptions regarding money and road life, it goes to one extreme or the other. Either we are absolutely wealthy or absolutely poor. Rich trust fund babies out on a joy ride with no jobs and unlimited daddy money or poor trailer trash hippies forced into bus life because we had no other options, living off Uncle Sam and handouts. The real answer is neither, at least for us. Bus life wasn't a last resort because we couldn't afford a home. We actively chose this path. Neither was it easy to attain; a lot of work and time and sacrifice went into building this life.

But it also isn't out of reach for most people who have a similar dream. We weren't better positioned financially compared to others around us to make it happen, and as you've read, we almost went upside down during the process. In other words, it's not only attainable for the super wealthy who have money to throw away, although for a build like ours, more money and work are required compared to simpler rigs with fewer luxuries.

It's important to note there are those within the nomadic community that do fit into those extremes, however. We've met people from all walks of life during our time as bus lifers, and certainly some who were either financially well-off and didn't need to work to afford pricey builds and travel or others using bus life as a way to make ends meet because other options were more expensive and unaffordable for them. The nomad community is a varied group with vastly different backgrounds and tax brackets. We've shared campfires with ex-Silicon Valley execs who retired early from six figure jobs and buskers who literally sing for their supper each night. Stock market traders and traveling artists. Successful businesspeople who take their office with them on the road and freelancers who depend on commissions to fill their tank. The draws of living nomadically appeal to people across every demographic. We've met people on multiple continents, of all different ages and ethnicities and race, with different levels of education and income and health, from all kinds of backgrounds and family situations. The common thread tying them all together is the road, and a willingness to live outside social norms to experience their dreams.

Similarly, those dreams manifest differently based on what they have available to them financially. Our build is considered a middle of the road kind of deal – we didn't have unlimited funds available, but we had enough to create a functional and beautiful space for ourselves with most of the luxuries one finds in a traditional home. Some builds are done over time, as funds become available, starting with a mattress on the floor and a camp stove. Some never evolve past what's absolutely necessary, with people relying on shower and bathroom facilities along the way. Some builds are hired out to professionals, with top of the line everything. Just like the people, the builds themselves span the gamut financially.

Another misconception along the financial vein is that of day-to-day life, and how expensive the living of bus life actually is. The most common assumption is that it's no cheaper than living in a traditional home and perhaps even more expensive with the rising costs of fuel. When people ask us what monthly expenses for bus life look like, it's hard to give a simple answer because as with the wide range of backgrounds and builds within the community, there's also a wide variety of ways people choose to live the lifestyle, and those choices create a pretty large range of answers. The monthly expenses of a giant bus versus a small van are different. A nomad who travels non-stop or stays in RV parks will have much higher living expenses than one who stays parked for longer periods of time or boondocks on free public lands free. Your fuel bill is entirely dependent on how much you travel and what kind of vehicle you have. We know nomads who only stay hooked up in RV parks and pay the equivalent of a small mortgage in fees, and others who have never paid for parking because they're entirely self-contained and stay out for weeks at a time between fill-ups.

In this case, again, I can only answer for us when I say bus life is vastly more affordable than our old lifestyle. Sure, gas isn't exactly cheap, but even during months of non-stop travel it's never exceeded our old mortgage. We no longer have monthly utilities to worry about, and we were able to pay off most of our debt after our home was dealt with, meaning no more credit card and car payments. Our main expenses each month are gas, insurance, and our phone bill. On the months we don't travel and stay parked, we take gas completely out of that equation. There are the additional considerations that pop up from time to time, like tires and engine maintenance, but they're not a constant and we're able to save and afford them out of pocket when they arise. This lifestyle allowed us to step out of debt and more than halved our monthly budget, meaning for the first time we were able to start saving huge chunks of our income instead of watching it fly out of our account just as quickly as it went in.

Another frequent concern is the issue of safety, both on the road and off. "That's all cool," they say, "But if you get in a wreck, you lose everything."

This isn't actually a complete misconception, to be fair. A wreck could be absolutely devastating if it was bad. But it is in that it's assuming a wreck equals the end of the line, the worst thing that could happen, a total loss. When this topic comes up, the conversation usually goes something like this one, pulled directly from my DMs with a friend.

"What if you get into an accident?" she asks.

"Well, that's why we have insurance. It would be sad, but I imagine we would just rebuild and get back on the road," I answer.

"But you lose everything you own!" she says, obviously horrified.

"Well yes, but that happens in regular homes too, right? My aunt's home burned down when her barbeque grill caught on fire, and we had to redo our basement once when a pipe broke and flooded it. No matter where you live, things can happen," I say.

"Yes, I guess you're right. I would just be so scared all the time."

"It's definitely something I think about, I won't lie. But when it comes to fear, I think I was more scared to stay in one spot and live the same day over and over, you know? One of my favorite quotes is, 'I would rather die on an adventure than live standing still', and for me that fear, the one where I'm not actually out living because I'm too afraid of what could go wrong, scares me more than what might go wrong while I'm chasing dreams and living a life I love."

We could wreck. It's a real concern. But school buses are tanks. They're meant to take kids safely to and from school, and after the chore of dismantling one, I trust the chassis my home is built in to withstand some serious destruction. It's actually one of the reasons we chose a school bus over an RV. After researching rollovers and collisions in both and seeing the differences between the two after a serious one, we felt far safer building our home in this metal tube on wheels. Car wrecks happen, and one day that might be an experience of our bus life. But I would rather risk one and know I was out living in a way that made me happy than have never chased this dream.

That safety translates off the road as well. We get hundreds of messages asking us if we feel safe parking in random locations at night, or if we're afraid the bus will get broken into, or if we've ever had issues with sketchy people trying to get in. I can honestly say I've never once, in over two years, felt unsafe in my little home. Parked out in the wild or in town, by myself or with Mike, this bus feels very much like a little bunker. I always chuckle and tell people it would take someone very determined to break into this bus. Yes, there's windows everywhere, but they're high up off the ground and small, with thick glass. We have a thick metal door on our metal clad home, and locks on everything. For me personally, I travel with a military trained martial artist who has a love affair with weapons of all kinds, many stashed away through the bus, and as a born and bred Montana girl, I've been able to shoot a gun accurately since I was a young teen. We also haven't personally heard any stories from bus lifers having issues like this. I'm sure it can and does happen, but the events are isolated enough they aren't a passed around concern in the bus life circles we've been a part of. To be fair, I have heard a story or two from some RV families about bears breaking into their rigs while they were out exploring, but no animals of the human variety.

One of my favorite misconceptions is that bus life really isn't all that great, that it's made out to be something it's not on social media. That it's not parking next to beaches and mountains every night, and that it's mostly Wal-Mart parking lots and emptying urine tanks and finding water fill-ups. Basically, that it's completely glamorized, and the reality is much more gritty and gross.

This one is hard to explain to people who aren't nomads. Because just like the misconceptions around safety, those assumptions are true in one way, but wrong in another. Once you've experienced it for a length of time, you get it. When we talk to fellow nomads about the joys of Wal-Mart parking lots, for instance, they nod and smile. They understand exactly what you mean. When you try to explain to someone who lives in a traditional home, it's hard for them to understand because their lifestyle is so different. However, I'm going to do my level best to communicate why this misconception is both accurate and completely wrong all at once.

As you've read, there are plenty of downsides to bus life. In other words, it definitely is not all sunsets over the ocean and coffee in the mountains. That is absolutely true. There are tanks to empty and fill, maintenance to consider, internet signals to chase for work, and yes, Wal-Mart parking lots. And those parking lots don't make it to a lot of social media posts, so in that way, this assumption is correct. As I mentioned before, I don't think this is purposely done to mislead anyone, I think it's just that whole highlight reel situation – pictures in parking lots just aren't as magical as ones with scenic vistas.

But those Wal-Mart parking lots are held near and dear in the heart of every single nomad I know. Some of our best nights have been spent in one, or something just like it. Not a gorgeous, bucket list destination, but a side of the road shoulder, a friendly restaurant or store lot, or a random rest stop with the truckers. Those less-than-Instagram-worthy overnight stops are loved and adored by road lifers. I can almost guarantee fellow nomads holding this book are nodding along and smiling as they read this, as a few specific blissful parking lot nights pop into their minds. For those without that perspective, however, let me try to explain.

When I lived in a traditional home, my vacation time every year was my only chance to experience something new and different. I loved getting away from home and staying in lovely locations, relishing luxurious hotels and Airbnbs and the scenery and experiences that went with them. I cherished each and every single one of those days away, packing as much into them as I could. If I'd had to spend any one of them at the travel equivalent of a Wal-Mart parking lot, like a cheap motel in a rundown part of town, I would have likely felt cheated of one of my precious days to live it up and enjoy my vacation.

When we moved onto this bus two and half years ago, however, our lifestyle changed. No more precious vacation days to experience everything we could in a short time frame; we can move around as we please, work from anywhere, and experience new things and beautiful places on a regular basis. The view from my office while I'm working is often beautiful scenery, and when I'm done for the day, I get to walk out and explore the sights I spent the morning appreciating while I worked. Whenever the mood strikes, I can have an adventure. There's no more pressure to fit everything into a few short, glorious weeks a year, because we now live and work very close to nature and new experiences. Even on the days we're at home base, the mountains and streams and lakes of Montana are within a half hour drive, and some days we literally take off and park somewhere nearby just to work for the day.

With my old mentality, I can clearly see how unglamorous parking in a Wal-Mart lot sounds. But with this new perspective, one where the majority of my life is spent enjoying it on a daily level in new places having experiences we love, they become something different, not something tolerated as necessary to the lifestyle, but something cherished and even looked forward to. Those parking lots are magical little adventures. They're a safe place to park in cities along our route. The novelty of pulling my home into the grocery store, walking in to restock for the next round of adventures, and then bringing my cart directly to the bus to unload still hasn't worn off. While the rest of the world bustles around us, stopping to shop and then hurrying back to their routines, we're making dinner with the fresh produce we just bought and watching everyone else go about their lives, the same way we used to.

In other words, bus life is one vast adventure, filled with all kinds of views and experiences and time spent in nature and exploring. Meaning parking in a Wal-Mart lot isn't just part of one bigger, grand trip, it's also offset against that larger picture. Even if we didn't actually enjoy nights in parking lots, bus life has given us so many other glorious ones they would still be worth it.

Of course, as I mentioned, misconceptions can run the other way too, disregarding the difficult parts and focusing only on the beautiful ones. In our experience, yes, bus life is much less stressful. There's a lot of freedom involved, and it creates space to grow personally in ways we didn't have room to before. But it doesn't change everything. Mike and I still fight from time to time. We still have stressful moments in our professional lives, days that feel overwhelming, problems that arise while traveling we have to deal with. Our kids still sometimes annoy us with their bickering, and there are times when we go to bed completely exhausted from a day gone awry. Bus life is not a stress free, blissful existence. And this perception, that there's no stress involved, and your life will overnight become one filled with non-stop rainbows and sunshine, is just as erroneous as believing it can't possibly live up to the hype. While the latter might stop you from chasing your dream, the former will lead to a lot of disappointed expectations. Jumping headfirst into bus life believing it's a cure all to life's stressors will likely lead to a hasty exit when you realize there are absolutely downsides and bad days.

The truth is, no matter the life you're in, it's mostly what you make of it. What you focus on is what you'll find more of – I believe bus life to be good, and for me, it mostly is. But I also know the pitfalls of our lifestyle, which means I'm prepared for them when they occur.

One of the most interesting things about misconceptions is that many of the people voicing them rarely remove themselves from their own perspective to even consider they might be making a hasty assumption with no actual knowledge of the topic that isn't accurate. It goes back to those boxes – human nature is to examine, decide, classify, and quickly file it away where further thought or need to examine is unnecessary. We want to understand the world around us, but we also don't want to understand any deeper than necessary within the scope of our own life experiences.

It helps me, when I'm dealing with those uninformed opinions, to remember the people who don't understand our choices are not really our people anyway, you know? They're not part of the community we're trying to build and foster and encourage and inspire. For some, it's because they don't understand, because they can't or don't want to wrap their head around a version of life different than their own; they're more comfortable in their misconceptions than sitting with the discomfort that arises from unanswered questions.

Filing something away as unsafe or unrealistic or not as awesome as it seems means they don't have to ponder it, wonder if they're missing out, or feel jealousy or sadness about it. They can simply dismiss it and carry on with their lives. And I do understand that urge. Once upon a time when I would see people living their best lives, it would make me uncomfortable, jealous and a little ashamed, even, knowing I wasn't doing the same, wasn't chasing my dreams. The difference, of course, is rather than leave nasty comments and assumptions for them, I used that discomfort to propel me forward into whatever it was I wanted. I feel a lot of gratitude for the people who cause me to feel moments of jealousy, because that envy, however uncomfortable, is a signpost for my brain to understand what direction my soul longs to go in.

Not to say that every mean or rude comment left comes from a place of jealousy. For some, it's simply the anonymity of the online world giving them a safe space to troll, typing out judgements they'd never say confidently to your face as they misplace whatever negative feelings they have with their own lives on you.

And finally, there's a group of people who are just not going to like you. We're inclined to be a fairly judgmental lot, aren't we? Combined with our penchants to assume and shove people into boxes, you can trust no matter what you do, someone, somewhere, will have an issue with it. As the unflappable Dita von Teese once said, "You can be the ripest, juiciest peach in the world, and there's still going to be somebody who hates peaches."

When we first started bus life, our Great Dane, Apollo, traveled with us, and we received comments all the time about what a shame it was our poor dog was cooped up in a bus. While we didn't feel bad about it at all, watching him run through forests and mountains instead of spending his life mostly in one yard, there were plenty of people who didn't agree and felt we shouldn't make a dog live on a bus. This last year, however, our old boy's dementia became a noticeable issue, and he wasn't able to travel with us anymore. Ironically, we now get hundreds of comments about how disappointing it is we don't have a dog or cat, and that we should adopt one from a shelter to give it a life exploring with us. The number of similar examples I could give, just since we started bus life, could fill another chapter of this book entirely.

"Why do you only photograph your home when it's clean, why not show us what real life looks like instead of this staged stuff all the time?" one says.

"Ugh, why is everything is everything immaculate except for your dash? That must be where the money ran out, I guess. Just clean your dash!" others cry on a video of our bus in motion.

"Post less exotic photos of yourself and show the downsides of this life," is left on a post of me sitting in the bus's side door, enjoying a cup of coffee.

"If I were able to live this life, I wouldn't complain about the sucky parts and would just be grateful," another commenter responds on a post detailing the requested downsides.

You will never, ever, as long as you live and try, find a way to make every single person happy. Most of us are lucky to get our entire family units to agree on what takeout to get for dinner, let alone finding a lifestyle choice or opinion the general masses as a whole approve of. I've come to realize no matter what I post, no matter what choices we're making or subject matter we're talking about or carefully thought out phrasing I use, someone, somewhere, will take issue and find their way into my comments and direct messages and texts.

And for some people, enough is never enough. We live in two hundred and fifty square feet of space on a school bus, and we've had people tell us that we aren't truly minimalists because there are people who live with even less. We once received a very angry direct message from someone who'd stumbled on our profile requesting we stop pretending we were minimalists, because we owned a television and a true minimalist wouldn't. We're vegan, reuse and recycle objects whenever we can, avoid single use items, make conscious purchasing decisions, grow our own food, and continue to search out ways to reduce our footprint on the earth, and still once had to block a completely irate follower who created new profiles to continue to harass us because we have a propane stove.

I say all this not to complain about our lot – it's our choice to live our lives out in the open, and I've long since quit caring what the people who don't understand us or our lifestyle think and say about us. You'll find those comments on our profile largely ignored, because I refuse to spend energy trying to change the opinions of people who have already come to their own conclusions, no matter how wrong they may be. I know my truths, and I'm secure in my decisions, lifestyle, and subsequent happiness. I used to feel like we owed explanations to people in choosing to share our lives on social media, even when they were overly personal or rudely worded.

Somewhere along the way, however, making myself half-crazy trying to thoughtfully respond to every single comment and email and direct message we received and explain our choices, I realized we don't owe anyone a damn thing. Especially in cases where the person on the other side of the screen can't even be bothered to ask their question in a polite way that shows they acknowledge they are, in fact, asking for answers to questions about the intimate details of my life that would be considered rude in general conversation, like how much money we make or how much our home cost.

While I don't mind answering these questions for people in order to help them make plans for their own dreams, I do take issue with those who demand the answers as if I'm withholding details they're owed. Call me picky, but I'm more inclined to answer a "may I ask how it is you and your husband are able to live this way and make money on the road" over a "how come you never answer questions about money, guess it must be a big secret you don't want to let anyone else in on" kind of question. Especially when the answer has been given thousands of times already across our platforms and website, if one can only be bothered to dig a little deeper than the singular post they happen to be viewing.

I'm also not saying this to the people who come to us with genuine questions based in misconceptions, the people who understand their beliefs may be faulty and are trying to gain knowledge to correct them. And I'm certainly not saying this to defend myself against the detractors of our lifestyle. If you don't get it, you don't get it, and I stopped banging my head on those metaphorical brick walls a while ago. As the saying goes, haters gonna hate, and when it comes to social media, trollers gonna troll.

Instead, I relay what we've learned on this topic for the

people still making themselves small to be less threatening to the small people around them. The sad fact of the matter is no matter what you do, no matter how well you phrase your thoughts and beliefs or lightly you try to tread, someone will find a way to take issue with it. I guarantee, someone reading this book or our social media, right now, is busy finding a way to take issue with it. But the silver lining of that rather bleak truth is there's freedom there, when you recognize this and stop trying to please others. When you realize there will always be someone who hates peaches, someone who can find fault in every action and inaction you take, your choice is to continue to pointlessly pander to the faceless masses trying to fit you into boxes, or to set yourself free to live in a way that makes you happy.

The world doesn't need more people confining themselves into ever-shrinking containers of what's acceptable, pulling their raw edges in tighter to take up less space. People have these strange rules they create for each other, where they feel everyone must think and feel and act the same way they do. It's scary, letting your freak flag fly, letting the vibrant colors of your soul show in a world that encourages gray conformity. And when you do, some people will absolutely mock you. They will question you and dismiss you and discourage you and even berate and belittle you, your choices somehow a threat to their life even when they in no way affect it.

But some other people, the ones who have niches in their soul that align with yours, won't. Those people will see the streaks of color, those unfurled living edges of your personality, and it will encourage them to show and embrace their own. And little by little, this world will become a more beautiful and colorful place, one filled with people running after their dreams, alive with possibility and no longer afraid. Perhaps those that mocked or questioned you will even one day come to you and ask you how you did it, finally willing themselves to travel a path they couldn't understand once.

Live your life friends, and speak your truth. Because while the misconceptions and assumptions may fly, at the very least you'll be enjoying the brief space of time we're given on this little blue planet, living a life that makes you feel more like yourself and, hopefully, inspires others to similarly chase their passions. Whether it's skydiving and traveling to every continent, or simply learning to knit or start a small vegetable garden in your backyard, this world would be infinitely more beautiful if there were more people living outside the misconceptions in order to dwell in places where passion and love reside.

Desert Sunsets

"Why do you want to go to the desert so badly?" he asked me.

"So I can see the stars," I replied.

(January 7, 2021)

It's still here, in the desert. I wasn't expecting to enjoy the landscape, much less fall in love with it. In my mind the idea of the desert has always been a wasteland, devoid of the life and color water provides. But I was wrong. The desert is alive and vibrant in a way the greener landscapes I'm so partial to aren't. And there's a quiet here the mountains and ocean can't touch, no babbling streams or rushing waves, no trees for the breeze to whistle through. There's just the silence, pushing against my ears as they strain for the tiniest whisper of sound. At night, I swear I can hear music in the hills, a melody that seems to come from somewhere in their depths. By day the landscape shimmers with heat, until it gives way to the velvet dark where billions of stars light up the infinite black depths of space. There's magic here.

There are lessons here too, for those who want to learn them. The vast landscape reminds me how absolutely small I am, as tiny in this universe as the individual grains of sand shifting under my bare feet are to the dunes they create. I feel utterly alone in the endless landscape, just Mike and I and a white bus named Oliver, and somehow, this comforts me. The only other souls around us are the tiny antelope squirrels bounding between the scrub brush and the watching hawks circling lazily overhead, and mine is at peace here with them.

For some reason, alone here as we are, it causes me to reflect on the many people who've entered my life. Thousands of casual conversations while waiting in a line or attending the party of a mutual friend, brief interactions with people I'd never meet again that somehow left a lasting impression I will always remember, people I assumed I would always be friends with whose role in the pages of my personal story instead abruptly ended. I find myself recalling them individually into the forefront of my mind, wondering how they are and where they've gone and if they're still the same people I once knew or ones I wouldn't be able to distinguish anymore.

I wonder if they would recognize me now, this curly haired woman lying on the roof of a bus under the stars. I think about the part I played in their stories and they in mine; hero and villain, confidant and enemy, lover and friend – I've danced many dances, played many roles. The people my recollections summon surprise me, faces I haven't seen in years and ones I shared only the briefest of interludes with. The shriveled and wizened old woman in the markets of Indonesia who held my hand and smiled when I asked if I could take her picture, my high school boyfriend rushing across a crowded dancefloor at prom to reach me as our song started playing, the friends who've held me while I've cried and others who told me I was too much or too little for them.

That's been a theme in my life, my too muchness and too littleness. For some, I am excessive, overboard, *a lot* to handle. For others I fall short, never quite enough. The boyfriend who told me he wished I could contain my spunk to the bedroom, because while he liked it there, he preferred I was less outspoken in our day to day lives. The friend who loved how generous and loving and forgiving I was when it came to her but didn't want me to give it away to others. My first love, who looked at me with eyes full of wonder and told me I was different from any other person he'd ever met, the same eyes that would look at me later full of disdain as he spat he wished I could just be more normal. They dance through my mind, these people I've known, the parts they've played in my story, however brief or long. I walk through the canyons, the breeze wafting the sweet smells of pinion and sage as I pause to pick up a tangerine quartz from the sand at my feet, the ghosts of my past close around me as I consider them from my current perspective.

Some left wounds I still nurse, scars that twinge around the edges when their faces unexpectedly pop into my mind. Others I miss with heavy longing, faces I ache to see just one more time. In some of their stories I am a hero, an inspiration, a catalyst. In others, I am absolutely the villain. All of them brought me lessons – in who I wanted to be, what I would and wouldn't tolerate in my life, what I respected and admired, and conversely, abhorred. Here in the desert, as the shadows of those I've known come to shimmer like mirages in front of me, the ones who linger are those I've loved most, the women who contributed the pieces of themselves I used to create this version of myself.

My childhood best friend, Charlotte, for instance. She's here with me, the same way she was as I watched my father die and my family fall apart. My polar opposite, calm to my chaos, and the rock I clung to during one of the most turbulent and terrible times of my life. She had everything I'd always wished to have, and rather than hold it close she shared it with me, including me in her family at a time I needed one most. She even shared her mom with me as my relationship with my own deteriorated; Bonnie taught me how to sew a quilt, bake bread, and not take any shit from anyone. Her daughter was my first example of quiet grace, a shy woman still utterly self-possessed, and to this day I admire the perfect blend of steely resolve and gentle sweetness that is my Charley.

My mentor, Sue, drifts in and out. She came into my life at the time I was most lost, as I crossed the threshold into my mid-thirties, when a few of the other faces floating through my mind's eye had recently departed and left me bereft and bitter. Suddenly there she was, a living, breathing version of the woman I hoped to someday become. Her long white curls tumbling around her as her hips sway to the music filling her book shop, alternating quick wit with deep empathy while she listens and nods, not giving you an answer but sitting with you while you come to your truth instead. The first time she hugged me, I felt peace all the way to my bones. She taught me about the magic in sadness and trees, what a rare and beautiful gift our time here is, and how to be a friend to myself.

My sister, Joniene, appears. When we leave this piece of the desert it will be to meet up with her, reunited after several years of absence to catch up in person. All I wanted in the world was to be just like her while I was growing up. She was so chic to me, so sophisticated and exotic with her dark curls and gray-green eyes. I used to sneak into her closet and steal her clothes so I could pretend I was as cool, and into her bed during stormy nights that scared me. She hated both, I'm sure, but she rarely showed it. In some ways she's still totally untouchable to me, elevated in my mind in only the way a big sister can be to a younger one, but what I'll find when I see her in a few weeks is that she and I are so much more similar than I'd ever realized when we were younger, and the joy that will fill my heart as she tours my bus and tells me she's proud of me will be something I carry with me for weeks after.

My mom is here with me, too. It took us many years for our relationship to finally mend. There's so much about her I never fully appreciated until life gave me opportunities to understand her perspective after experiencing it from my own. Becoming a mother made me realize how truly hard she always tried, even when I felt she'd failed me at the time. Our relationship went quickly south when she remarried after my dad's death; I thought her cowardly for rushing into the arms of another man instead of being resolute enough to forge her own way. When I got married myself, however, and thought about losing him to a disease, watching him waste away and die in my arms, I was humbled. I can only stand in awe now at the courage it took her to imagine a new life for herself after the one she'd planned was wrenched from her grasp, at her bravery in loving again. My mother has plenty of flaws, and just like she and her mother before her, I find myself sometimes muttering to my husband, "If I ever become like my mother, shoot me."

But my mother is also one of the kindest people I know, and has grown into an entirely different person from the one of my childhood years. She puts the people she loves far before herself, constantly going out of her way to make sure they're cared for and feel her love in a way that sometimes devastates her own boundaries. In spite of the myriad of heartache she's borne in her life, she opens hers time and again to people; life and its tragedies has not made her heart hard, it's made it bigger.

And so we dance, here in the desert under the stars, the people I've loved and learned from. Mike remarks I'm quieter here, and I reply I'm enjoying the space and don't want to fill it. He smiles, silent himself in his own musings as we walk among the scrub toward a lone Joshua tree silhouetted on the ridge behind the bus. Their faces flash in my mind, and I allow the rush of emotions each brings to linger, feeling them fully. I realize the vastness around me offers more than enough space for my lifetime of hurts and hopes to spread out where I can more fully examine them, room for the parts and pieces of themselves people have left with me to tumble from the recesses of my mind. Under the desert sun I can see them more clearly, and I spend my days there mostly in silent contemplation, ruminating over the people who've come in and out of my life and the lasting effects, good and bad, of their presence in it.

We are, none of us, entirely good or bad. We are all both light and dark, victim and aggressor, lover and fighter. We never know, when the strand of someone else's life meets with ours, how they will come together. Our stories are woven together with the borrowed threads of others, a patchwork of different shades and tones creating the ever-widening tapestry that is an individual life. Only at the end of it are we able to look back and see the finished fabric, how the fibers we used worked together, whether they complimented each other or created snags in the weft.

The morning we packed up to leave the desert and head back into the mountains, I walked outside as the sun rose dusty pink over the white sand. I stood cloaked in a blanket, the predawn air frigid cold on my face. There was no sound, just the dark and quiet cocooned around me as tightly as the throw I clutched to my shoulders. The world slowly lightened as the golden disc appeared, shimmering on the skyline with the first heat of the day. I watched it climb steadily upward, until, with a final leap, it jumped above the horizon. The blanket slipped from my shoulders to fall at my feet, and as it did, I realized it wasn't the only thing shedding off me in this new day. My face turned upward to the sun, I released all the emotions I'd allowed to come up to the surface while we were here to now fall to the ground as well.

Lingering shame and regrets, the pain of past hurts, one by one they fell from my shoulders to the desert floor. As each came up, I saw the face that went along with it, the people I'd hurt and been hurt by, and felt nothing but love and gratitude for their part in my life and the lessons they'd helped me learn. I sent silent prayers up for them; that they, too, felt healing, and could forgive me for the wrongs I'd done them as well. I waited until I felt the last of these emotions slough off, as the sun continued to climb higher in the sky, until only its heat remained on my skin and the mirages that had kept me company in this lonely place evaporated into the morning with the dew.

I bent and picked up my blanket, leaving the rest on the dusty ground, and turned to the bus where Mike was walking out the front door with a steaming mug of coffee for me, a new woman in the new day, ready for a new adventure.

Bus Life in the Time of Covid

I'm not going to lie - we came back to the grid yesterday hesitantly. After a week of doing nothing but this, celebrating our eight-year anniversary (a little early), we were loath to leave it behind. We spent the week laying in this hammock, reading and connecting over too many cups of coffee to count. We baked cherry pies that we ate for breakfast, walked together in that ice cold creek behind us, and had picnics that faded into watching the stars appear between the treetops.

Mostly, we talked. A lot. About the world around us, what we've seen in our almost nine years together, what we're experiencing collectively now. We felt into the situations and stories that have surrounded us the last few weeks. Brainstormed ways to move forward, places that light needed to shine and how to be a conduit for it.

I think we are all looking at the world around us right now, then looking at ourselves and trying to discern our place in it. A hard enough task in a world not on fire, and an almost impossible one in the scope of our current climate, where no matter what you believe you will find vehement opposition telling you that you're wrong.

Even so, despite not fully wanting to leave and knowing what we are coming back to, we came out of those woods with lots of ideas and plans and, above all else -

hope.

We have a lot to share. We are, by trade, writers, and that's what we do here - we share stories. Some of those stories won't change. This is, after all, an account detailing the lives of two digital nomads living in a bus. But we have other stories to tell now beyond our tiny home. They are stories about this period of time and the world this little bus rumbles around in.

We hope you'll find value in them all.

(June 15, 2020)

W hen the world locked down and locked up at the beginning of 2020, the skoolie community was one of the groups uniquely prepared for it. Our children already homeschooled, our jobs already online, our homes already isolated, our lifestyle already mostly socially distanced. While friends and family dealt with the new challenges of working at home and helping kids adjust to online classes and not going out for those weekly coffee dates and weekend shopping trips, the island we'd built for ourselves in the form of a school bus didn't even feel a passing ripple.

And I'm not going to lie, I was profoundly grateful for the calm waters we rested in as others dealt with wave after wave of change in their lives, trying to keep everything afloat. We would often talk over coffee in the morning, imagining what our lives would look like if we still owned the gym, ending each conversation with a sigh of thankfulness to be in the place we are now instead.

This is saying something in that it wasn't just Covid that rocked the planet. Five years after the point Mike and I initially started waking up in our own lives, people around the globe found themselves looking at the world around them anew. After all, this was 2020, the year we all stood still, when markets fell to viruses and humanity was forced to take a collective halt only to reemerge to a landscape of protests and unrest and looming elections and mandates. People who'd never had time or space to question their routines and life choices suddenly found themselves at full stop, looking at the minutiae of daily life and how they spent their time. New hobbies were born, routines were changed, and in many cases, a more thoughtful and intentional life was built in place of ones that had been on autopilot for years. People found perhaps they didn't want a complete return to normal and preferred the space and quiet this forced pause gave them. The second decade of this century, as my Gen Z daughter would say, hit different.

The news blares sensationalized stories, different versions of the same tale depending on which network you're tuned into. The truth must be out there, but trying to find it wading through thousands of stories screaming their biased headlines seems more difficult than the proverbial needle in a haystack. Some cope with this by tuning out entirely, going about business as usual until they're forced to pay attention when their Facebook feed is flooded with memes about the next big thing everyone else is upset about. Some do the opposite, letting their disgust and rage fuel a headlong sprint toward extremism that leaves them tuning into the news once an hour so they can shake their head and repost every meme they find supporting their ideologies.

When we were younger, we were told it was bad form to sit on a fence, that one needed to pick a side and know where they stood and not "be a fence-sitter". As an adult, I now respectively and vehemently disagree with this notion. Don't get me wrong – there are times when it becomes absolutely necessary to choose a side, times when your moral compass should dictate you stand absolutely and resolutely against whatever is on the other side of the fence.

The problem is the line where this occurs varies for people. Most would agree murder is bad, but the line immediately gets blurry. A pro-life advocate will tell you abortion is murder. A vegan will tell you your burger is. And here's the thing – in their minds, with their beliefs and awareness and perceptions and experiences, they're each right. But in each of these situations, I promise you there is someone with different held beliefs and lived experiences who would read those sentences and disagree. A pro-choice advocate will argue about when life becomes viable and bodily autonomy. A meat-eater doesn't see animals as equal to himself, but as master of them, and therefore subject to his whims.

Who is right?

This brings me back to that fence we were always told not to sit on, and why I've decided to put a saddle on that thing and ride it through every situation I possibly can. The fence is midway. It's being able to see down onto both sides of it and recognize both the beautiful and the ugly on each. In other words, the fence is the best view of any situation. The problem when we step down onto one side or the other is our view of the entire field of thought becomes blocked. If we're still near the fence, we might be able to at least see through the slats and have conversations with people on the other side.

But once we're down on one side, what is available for us to see and hear is largely confined to the information on our chosen side as the other becomes muted. We've put ourselves into an echo chamber, where the information we're able to see and hear is what we already believe to be true. Our beliefs are no longer challenged, we're no longer asked to consider the other side; instead, as we mingle with others on this side of the fence, our beliefs are simply echoed back to us and reinforced in a way that cements how absolutely right we must be, because everyone here agrees with us.

And this is where the trouble starts.

We start taking in only one side of the story. We forget the very valid points and views the other side may have had that are in opposition to the ones we've embraced as gospel truth, the ones that actually help form the whole and more complete picture. Our information is limited, which means our thinking follows suit. We start taking steps away from the fence as our beliefs become more rooted in this side, and in a nasty cycle, this in turn cuts us off even more from the other side. Not only can we no longer see the other side, we start to forget there are people on that side we could once talk to and identify with in other ways. They become the enemy, a presence we can't even tolerate and must belittle because we are now so mired in our side's views, we can't imagine anything outside of them. Then the screaming starts, bellowing across the field and yelling our new views at the top of our lungs in hopes those on the other side will hear and climb over to join our righteous stand on this side of the fence, the side of our perceived truth and justice.

Funny how both sides are absolutely sure they alone possess the complete truth of the matter, isn't it?

The final step of this is extremism, the people who are now

so far from the fence they see the other side as evil and hateful and a threat to be exterminated. This is where wild conspiracies and destructive plans are born, the place where people go all in, not just tumbling down the rabbit hole but actively digging deeper, their vitriol palpable as they proceed to alienate their friends and families with non-stop memes about how stupid everyone else is and when will everyone just WAKE UP?!?!

To be fair, this is actually the point where the next, ever-evolving level of said waking up happened for me, although not in the way the angry people hoped, perhaps – the day I realized the people riding the fence seemed to be the sanest among us and chose to join them. The fence-sitters are those who can stand with one foot in either camp and argue both sides of the issues, being the only ones able to see the entire field of view, after all, from their perch. They're the moderates, the ones checking out from the news to spend more time with the people they love and less time being angry at the theater playing out in the news between talking heads. The ones who recognize reposting memes on social media and constantly bombarding their friends and families with regurgitated rhetoric is as futile an endeavor as expecting anyone in a position of power within that media or the government it reports on to actually tell the truth to we the people as the pendulum of democracy swings us frequently between sides, bringing changes every cycle.

The funny thing is, after typing all that out, thinking back on all the fear and anger that played out over the last year, I don't feel despair. Once upon a time, I did. There was a period where I definitely became caught up in it, where I swear I must have thought "what in the ever-loving hell" at least once an hour doom-scrolling the news, looking up to Mike and reading a headline followed with the words "I'm losing all hope in humanity right now" daily. But curiously enough, as it tends to, that period of discomfort and fear and anger triggered another of growth and understanding and acceptance. Not of the world, necessarily, but of my place in it, and where my energies are best directed. I'd started to believe I must care all the time about every single issue at hand in order to be a good human, as if only dedicating my energy to the issues my heart felt truly pulled to made me somehow less caring instead of realizing we are all here with unique callings laid on our souls.

I cannot single-handedly change the opinions and beliefs of an individual rooted into them, let alone the myriad of problems the world is plagued with. My anger and disgust and fear will only be met with and spawn more of the same. You will not change the minds of those around you by yelling at and belittling them, spreading hate and anger and hurt in a world already so heavy with it. You may rile people up, you might cause them to pause and consider, but ultimately, most people don't come to a genuine change of heart because they were screamed at or mocked.

What does change hearts and minds, every time, is love. It's always been amazing to me, what just a little bit of the stuff can do. To my mind, love is the single most powerful force on the face of this planet, both good and bad. It moves us to war over love of our countries and religions and freedoms, to change our entire lives when we fall headfirst into it, and to become better people in the face of it. Look at the number of people who changed destructive habits because someone entered their life and finally gave them a reason to, who raise large amounts of money to help those they love or start charities to honor someone they lost, who sacrifice their own happiness to create it for others, and you'll begin to see how magnificent the gravity of the emotion we call love is. It inspires and destroys, builds and disrupts. But above all, it heals in a way only time rivals.

The one truly positive thing I can say about 2020 is that during the collective pause, where we all took stock of our lives and what they contained, we happened to find our next big dream, the one that made sense to us both in terms of where we, personally, and the world at large were heading. It wasn't a conscious thought, there was no big buildup or planning, it just developed naturally over time as we sat waiting for the world to breathe again. When the year that brought the world to a halt began, we were just bus lifers chasing the next horizon and not making plans too far into the immediate future. But as the new one dawned, we suddenly found ourselves smack dab in the middle of building a new life, one we hadn't foreseen but made perfect sense for the world and where we were in it. The Feral Homestead was born.

Feral Homestead

Living with me is always an adventure, as both my former and current husband like to say. For instance - when we decided to hunker down here over the summer thanks to Covid, I told my first husband we should plant a garden in his neglected backyard. He laughed and said whatever I wanted, and so we quickly threw in a late garden (it was almost June).

For the first 6 weeks, nothing seemed to grow. It was like it was stunted. Seeds took weeks to germinate, and when they finally did, they stayed suspended as seedlings for weeks.

I was reading a book about Perelandra at the time, and gardening in companionship with Nature. Over dinner one night, I brought up what I'd read earlier in the week - about plant energy and how they're affected by ours, and in this case, how maybe ownership of the land mattered.

I told the boys maybe the garden wasn't growing because technically Evan owned the land, not me, and he needed to release it to me for the garden to thrive under my care.

They laughed. I was deathly serious (as serious as I ever am) and leveled my most unamused gaze at him. And so right there at the dinner table, humoring me, Evan threw his arms wide and yelled, "I hereby give my backyard to Tawny!", and we all started howling.

That same week the garden finally took off. And today, it's a veritable jungle producing so many pounds of produce we can hardly keep up. Energetic finagling or coincidence I don't know, but the boys still laugh about it every night while we're out scouting for the day's offerings.

I'm putting snippets of my garden this morning in my stories today, if you care to walk the jungle with me.

Welcome to life with Tawny. I live in a bus, I talk to my plants, and life with me is never boring. Also, I am apparently now steward of this large backyard.

(August 13, 2020)

That's the real and true story of how the Feral Homestead started in my ex-husband's backyard. Of course, at the time, we didn't know it was the beginning of our next chapter, a new dream we'd soon be chasing. At that point, it just made sense, a project to keep my easily bored mind busy while we paused travel. As Covid emerged and we were all encouraged to stay home, we'd decided it would be prudent to stick close to our families and hometown in case even more upheaval occurred, especially as public lands closed down and parking dwindled.

And so we planted a hasty garden in the overgrown weed patch that was Evan's backyard and put down some literal roots for the first time in a year. It felt odd, to not have any travels planned, but also nice to have a safe place to just be while the world grew ever more chaotic by the day. This was during the point I'd gotten briefly into that doom-scrolling mentality, and like many others, began asking questions about the fragility of our systems and our dependence on them. As grocery aisles started coming up bare and shortages hit commodity items, the garden that had been a whim suddenly seemed incredibly important. After all, should the shelves at the grocery store stay bare, what would we do?

Long talks happened during those early summer evenings, rehashing the day's news stories and reflecting on their possible future outcomes and significance to our lives. Mike and Evan and I started looking forward, imagining a more sustainable and self-sufficient way of life that would allow us to release reliance on the corporate systems that, while convenient, left us vulnerable to their success or failure. In other words, if the supply chains we relied on for food and water and power and commodities were interrupted, how would we provide for our family?

We started forming new plans. We didn't want to stop traveling, but in the same way we'd discovered just a month or so before we were happier to remove ourselves from the "have bus must travel" box, we realized with our unique situation, parked with family, we had the option to create a home base for ourselves that was more than just a simple parking spot. Starting right then, right where we were, with what we had available, we could create a more sustainable future for ourselves. Not all dreams need a complete upheaval of the life you're currently living to begin. Some just need a little space inside the one you already have. Converting a bus into a tiny home and transitioning to life on the road required us to abandon one path completely for another, but this, creating a homestead in order to be more self-sufficient, simply required we merge two similar paths. The bus had already given us a level of freedom we hadn't been able to imagine even while building it; while putting down any kind of literal roots at first seems to run completely perpendicular to that freedom, it actually creates another kind of independence that aligns perfectly. And we aren't the only ones who think so. There are a large number of skoolie, RV, and van lifers who ultimately buy land to create a similar setup for themselves. Even without Covid throwing wrenches into our travel plans, we've realized we likely would have come to this point anyway as the next logical step of our journey.

In any event, starting in the summer of 2020, we spent every moment of free time between travels building the foundation of our new little home base. The full realization of our dream was a large piece of land completely removed from the grid, a blank slate to build and create a self-sustainable homestead using permaculture practices. But we weren't going to make the mistake of waiting for that perfect slice of heaven on earth to appear before we started.

So many people, when they have a dream, hesitate to move on it, waiting for a perfect combination of elements to occur. Sometimes I think that's part of what separates the dreamers who only ever fantasize from the dreamers who actually create. Those who actually live their dreams in real life are the ones who don't wait for a perfect situation to occur before chasing them. They're the ones up late at night after their day job is done working a side hustle toward their future, not waiting until they have enough money saved up to be able to pursue the dream with nothing else on their plate. They're the people you see carving out bits of time and money and space wherever they find it in their lives to slowly build toward their hoped-for future instead of saying, "One day after _____ happens, I'll finally have (time, money, etc.) to do that thing I want to do so badly."

Whether it was starting a business, training for competitions, teaching ourselves new skills or languages, or building a bus, Mike and I are people who go for what we want. Over and over in our lives, people have asked us how we did whatever it was they were similarly dreaming of – what inspired us to start, what made us jump in, how we learned what to do or where our confidence came from to get started. The point we always try to relay to those asking is that we are in no way special. We didn't have extra money, we didn't have special skills, and we very rarely had time laying around to just pick up something new to start. Every single dream we've pursued has come at the cost of sacrificing something else to free the time and money and energy it required. Sometimes that was sleep and sanity and time together, like in the nursing school days when we worked alternating nights from each other at the hospital in order to be able to get our classes done during the day before kids got home from school. Sometimes it was any spare time and money we had, as we built our gym in our backyard every night and weekend after a full day's work. In the case of the bus, as you've read, we gambled and sacrificed every single part of the life we'd painstakingly built from the ground up over the previous five years on this dream called bus life.

When people ask you how you did it, how you arrived at a place they hope to be, you'll mostly get two kinds of responses. The first group will ask you more questions, as they formulate how they too might be able to sacrifice and commit pieces of their lives to the dream, starting right where they are, with what they have available. The second group will begin to relay reasons they wouldn't be able to make those same sacrifices or commitments, and say things like "someday" and "when this happens I will be able to dive in" and "I just don't know if I could do that".

I watched my dad die in front of me of cancer when he was in his forties. Since that time, I've said goodbye to an uncle who hadn't yet reached thirty when he was in a horrific car accident, a fellow personal trainer who was just older than me at thirty-three when he was beaten to death in a fight, and one of my favorite training clients who lost his battle with lifelong depression around the same age. In other words, I know someday isn't guaranteed. When that second group says someday, I always say a little prayer they're allowed to see it, and with it, their dreams. But I will never wait on a someday because I've seen too many taken abruptly away to tuck my dreams away into them.

And so, in Evan's large backyard, we spent our time laying the foundation of this new dream. Our practice run, we called it, as we continued to keep an eye out for a larger piece of land meeting our criteria much the same way we'd searched for the perfect bus just a few years before. Nothing much had ever been done with the yard in the interim time between when Evan and I had built the house and Mike and I came to park at it. The backyard was fenced, containing nothing but weeds, random debris from years of inside projects, and a rundown shed full of mice. After a good deal of cleaning and clearing, we were left with a rather drab blank slate we spent the remainder of the summer filling. The overgrown weed patch became neat rows of garden beds. The shed, once repaired and renovated, was turned into a small barn to house the growing number of animals we slowly collected. And, little by little, project by painstaking project, a backyard turned into a tiny sliver of our dream, a little peek of what the future could hold to tide us over while we continue chasing the larger one.

When we named our gym, it took us a long time to find the perfect moniker. We settled on The Asylum, which held a dual meaning for us. As I mentioned before, we joked because people were always telling us we were crazy when it came to fitness, getting up at three in the morning to work out before we had to train others or working out multiple times a day to prepare for competitions, we needed an asylum to be "committed" to. As a matter of fact, that was our tagline on apparel and merchandise we sold. But asylum also carries the connotation of a safe haven too, and that's what physical fitness was for us, something we could pour ourselves into even on our worst days and walk away feeling better, a way of life that healed and inspired us to be better. The Asylum was so named as a tribute to all the gym and that way of life had been to us.

When we decided our tiny, burgeoning, urban homestead needed a name, we instead chose one that encompassed our future dreams for it, everything we hoped it would be, a reminder – the Feral Homestead. Existing in a wild condition, returning to an untamed state after domestication. When we meet up with other road lifers, we often joke among ourselves we're the feral ones in society, returning to our rolling homes with dirty feet and smudged faces after a day of adventures, crowded around campfires comparing stories of the places we've explored and how we'll never return to a house with a neatly trimmed yard again.

And I don't think most of us ever will. We've tasted too much freedom living unchained from the nine to five, dancing under stars and swimming in forest streams, to ever want to return to domesticated life again. We've become as untamed as the wild lands we love to traverse. And that's my hope for this new dream we're building. A home base for us where we live in sync with the land and her cycles, a place where our wild meets the land's. A homestead I hope will never be totally tame, where the forest is always just at risk of overtaking the garden and disappearing into nature means a short walk out the front door.

Today, the start of the Feral Homestead is really just a very large backyard given to me one night at a dinner table in an impromptu ceremony of bellowed words. But it doesn't make it any less magical to me. What was once meant to be a landscaped and manicured backyard has become a vast tangle of growth instead. Vines and bushes full of fruits and vegetables create a veritable jungle, overgrown paths studded with mushrooms between them. Hundreds of bees and dragonflies flit from plant to plant, filling the air with a steady hum of wings, frogs and snakes scarpering out of the way when you pass. Beyond the maze of plants, in the grass where a flock of birds range around, you'll find nests holding clutches of multicolored eggs beside a pond.

What we've started on this small piece of land will continue to grow here, and someday, what we've planted will take root and be the groundwork of the next chapter in this story. As we sit on our little front porch or around the fire pit in the evenings, surveying this tiny kingdom, I don't think of that chapter, however. I simply see the work, how far we've come, what we've managed to do so far with a full heart. I think back on the early months of 2020, those conversations we had worrying about our future, and feel profound gratitude to no longer hold any anxiety surrounding possible outcomes. And to be honest, I feel a lot of pride in what we managed to accomplish in the last year since we had those talks around a dinner table.

A large garden provides more produce than we sometimes know what to do with. We do successive plantings and built a small greenhouse, which means even in Montana we have at least a few things growing year-round. An herb garden supplies all manner of goodies for natural remedies and teas and body care. The small barn now holds a flock of various birds named after Harry Potter characters, including a rooster named Neville who proved not to be a rooster one day when she started laying eggs (but the name stuck) and a turkey named Lavender we rescued from being someone's Thanksgiving dinner, after I swore I wouldn't get a turkey, because she happens to be the best cuddler of any animal I've ever met and I couldn't say no after she curled up and fell asleep trustingly in my arms after being neglected and left behind by her previous owner. They're joined by three Nigerian dwarf goats, Maple, Mocha and Mac, who like to liven the place up by bleating loudly when you forget to bring them treats from the garden and playing king of the mountain on the large wooden spools we've placed in the animal yard, rearing up and cracking their heads together over and over until one finally gives up and jumps down. Keeping them, besides entertainment and snuggles, means we have a fresh supply of milk and eggs.

We've also spent time honing skills necessary to homestead

life. I resurrected old hobbies from when the kids were young, and began spinning and weaving and knitting again, creating blankets and clothing. Mike picked up blacksmithing, and true to form, began almost immediately turning out beautiful and functional tools and lovely pieces of jewelry, and we now sell these handmade items at a local store. We started canning and preserving in order to save every precious offering from our garden, making a root cellar in Evan's basement to store the supply of food. This fall, lines of canned goods and bags of grains will be stacked neatly under ropes of dried onions and garlic and beside bins of squash and root vegetables. Besides alleviating the worries we once had about providing for our family in the event something interrupted the world as we know it, the skills we've learned and life we've created parked here have given us true joy and satisfaction.

That's not to say we don't relish traveling every opportunity we get. Parking here with family means when our itchy feet tell us it's time to do some wandering, we can take off knowing everything here will be cared for until our return by equally invested people who also enjoy the satisfaction it's created for them. While this wasn't what we imagined when we were building the bus, not waking up to a new location every week, I can't say I mind. I would have, perhaps, if you'd told me at the time, but like so many things, theory and practice are two very different things. I wanted sunrises and sunsets over new horizons when we first started, but watching the sun set and rise over this little piece of homestead heaven we've created is just as satisfying as the many glorious ones we've witnessed in locations all over the world now. Neither better or worse, just different types of joy to be found in each.

I will never turn down the opportunity to travel to a new destination. Walking down a road my feet have never been before, seeing and touching and breathing and tasting something new, will probably always be my favorite experience in life, and I hope there are thousands more of them before my eyes dim and energy fails. But living in this bus has given me such a beautiful gift of perspective, the experience of so many new roads, that when we arrive at this familiar one, I feel nothing but gratitude to turn down it once more and find ourselves again in a backyard turning slowly more and more feral.

My Greatest
Adventure

We get a lot of DM's asking about our family situation and how we make it work. I don't really have an answer to that, except lots of love and respect. But let me try to explain it better for those who asked.

Evan and I met when we were 21 and 18. Of course, at this tender age, we knew exactly who we were and what we wanted out of life. The short story is that we were brilliant friends and parents, but our completely opposite personalities warred more often than not.

When we separated, however, love and respect still remained and we agreed on one thing above all else - no custody battles, no courts. The kids were priority one. Mike entered the picture shortly after, and while there was an adjustment period, he became part of that arrangement.

Today we all parent together. Mike and Evan are best friends who work out together every night and laugh at each other's dad jokes. When we travel, they get to choose whether to stay with dad or go with us. Sometimes we all travel together.

We also have a permanent parking spot at Evan's that allows us to have our own space while all dwelling in the same space, an arrangement that gives the kids the best of all worlds. We go shopping together, eat dinner together every night, and generally all work together on a daily basis.

I give full credit to Mike and Evan for how we work - I love incredible men with selfless hearts. And my children are evidence.

(August 29, 2020)

It's lucky we settled so naturally into parking with Evan, and building a home base with him, because this was also the year our kids stopped traveling with us. As they were starting to prepare for high school exams, they very gently informed us that traveling in a bus doesn't hold appeal for them any longer, and they preferred to stay with their dad rather than crisscross the US in an old school bus. It was a little sad to accept, but we knew from day one this would come. After all, we started bus life when they were already in their teens, that time in our lives when we're trying to separate ourselves from our parents and require inordinate amounts of personal space. I simply feel grateful for the time we were able to share this tiny home rather than being focused on how short it seems looking back.

And Mike and I don't mind being able to take off, just the two of us. Being alone together has been a long-anticipated dream of its own. But we do miss them when they aren't here.

It's the conundrum of the empty nest – relieved to have space and time of your own as an individual once more, enjoying the freedom, but also not quite sure what to do with yourself now it's arrived and missing the young people you raised who are suddenly self-sufficient.

Many people who follow us online are actually surprised to learn we have kids at all, because they're rarely shown on our social media. When I first began sharing our lives online, they were featured heavily. But after a short time, we made a conscious decision to no longer include them in those spaces. A few major news outlets wrote some articles about our conversion and lifestyle. While you'll always find a mix of good and bad in the comments section, our own social media and many places we're shared online, like tiny home profiles, are mostly the former. When your audience is targeted people following a specific niche they're interested in, you'll receive mostly support and love for what you share. These articles, however, were in massive publications not targeted to a specific audience, and there were a higher number of thoughtless and rude comments left under the articles.

Not as equipped as young teens to deal with others' judgement of their lifestyle as Mike and I were as adults, they read through the comments criticizing our lifestyle and making rash generalizations with growing indignation. Their outrage on our behalf when we were called terrible parents for making our kids live in a bus, or when others surmised I must be a drug addict or deadbeat mom to not have full custody of my children, not pausing to consider I would still have a shared custody arrangement even if I lived in a traditional home situation, was actually quite heart-warming. While it wasn't a happy experience for them, I was actually grateful for the conversations that came from it. We had long discussions about judgement and ignorance, how we can't really understand what another person's experiences are until we've actually lived them, and how continuing patterns of behavior only leads to a never-ending circle of the same, while meeting anger with compassion can instead break the cycle.

That experience changed their perception, not of our experience, but of their place in it. Not long after, they respectfully asked I no longer post photos and videos of them. It was one of the most adult conversations I'd ever had with my kids, as they explained their decision was both for their own privacy and because that way, we wouldn't have to field ignorant comments from judgmental people about the merits of our parenting and chosen lifestyle. I will never forget how impressed I was in that moment, at their fierce protectiveness of us as parents, their higher understanding of the situation, and how they respectfully set boundaries for themselves about what they would and wouldn't accept.

It reminds me of when they learned Santa Claus wasn't real. We'd decided it was time to tell them the truth rather than allow them to learn from classmates and friends, as my younger brother who is a few years older than them tragically had, with devastating results for my parents. We took time to write out a carefully composed letter, explaining the true joy and meaning behind Christmas. It took us days to come up with just the right words, thoughtfully constructed, as we anticipated ruining the magic of the man in the red suit with trepidation. When the night came, we gave them the letter and stood by as they read it, waiting apprehensively for their reactions. When they finished, Ely carefully folded the letter and looked with a smirk at her brother.

"Do you want to tell them or should I?" she asked.

"Tell us what?" I spluttered, completely nonplussed at this breezy reaction.

"Well mom," she carefully started, as if explaining gently to five-year-old why they can't have ice cream for dinner, "We've actually known for some time that Santa isn't real, and that you guys get us the presents."

"How did you know?" Mike choked out, his shock as palpable as mine.

"Well, Aidyn found our Easter baskets hidden in your

closet a few years ago, and we figured if the Easter bunny wasn't real, Santa couldn't be either," she answered.

"Why didn't you tell us?" By this point my voice had raised a few octaves, shrill with disbelief as the tables of new discoveries were turned on us. I'd been so pitying of them only moments before, about to dash their childhood beliefs, but it was our kids who now raised eyes full of pity toward us.

Aidyn looked at his sister, and then patiently answered. "Well, it just seemed to make you all so happy to be Santa that we didn't want to ruin it for you guys."

After that article and the talks that came with it, the only photos and videos occasionally appearing are those they've approved beforehand, generally posts about our family dynamic with Evan. This isn't to say I think it's wrong for parents who post photos and videos of their kiddos online to do so. There have been so many times I've wished to share a particularly stunning image or a funny anecdote from my own, and I love seeing the photos and posts of our friends' children. But as they'd obviously put a good deal of thought into their respectful request, I honored it as what's right for our family.

When I was writing this book, however, there was also no way I could similarly leave them out. Especially since it was these two souls I was gifted, the ones who call me mom, who were one of the catalyzing factors that pushed us into bus life. I can't write a book about our adventures in bus life and leave two of the lead characters out. They may not be featured on our social media, but they've been just out of the frame of so many of those posts.

Aidyn was born when I was a child myself, barely out of school. His dad and I were still strangers in so many ways; our son was conceived after only three months of dating, and he entered the world almost a year to the day we'd met. I bawled hysterically when I took that pregnancy test, sure my life was over as this new path suddenly appeared before me. My friends were finishing their first year of college, and I was suddenly *that girl*, the one with the unplanned pregnancy dropping out instead. The first few months were terrible, as morning sickness and emotions roiled through my belly. But when I was five months pregnant, both the physical and emotional nausea finally passing and having resigned myself to motherhood, something happened I wasn't expecting. I fell in love.

Evan and I shared a car back then, so every morning around five I would drive him in to work and then take my quickly growing belly back home to bed for a few hours. The traffic was sparse in the early hours of the day, hardly anyone on the road around me as I made my way back home one unremarkable fall morning. One of my favorite Coldplay songs thrummed from the speakers as I waited for a stoplight to turn green, eager to regain the warmth of our bed. Just as Chris Martin crooned he'd bleed himself dry for the person he loved, the baby kicked me for the first time. Not a little flutter, not a small movement, but a solid, sudden kick. My hand moved to my belly, and for the first time, I realized there was an actual human being inside me, a real person. My son.

Tears coursed down my cheeks as lyrics about love wrapped around us. Because there *were* two of us here now, suddenly, in this car. He and I. The light turned green and then red again as I sat there, arms clasped around my belly, sobbing as I sang to him and his little feet pressed against me, dancing to the song that would forever bring me back to this moment with him, the one I became a mom in my heart. Since that moment, he's owned a piece of mine.

I finally met him in person four months later. He entered the world after a bit of a kerfuffle; thirteen hours of labor produced no results to my cervix, and an ultrasound revealed my pelvic bone was tipped backwards, not allowing his head to engage. A caesarean was quickly scheduled, and it all moved so fast after that the details are blurry to me now. What I do remember is them having to poke me with the massive epidural needle multiple times while the anesthesiologist repeated, "Just a little bee sting!" over and over, because my belly was so massive by that point, I couldn't bend far enough over it to properly separate my vertebrae into position.

But he was worth it. I couldn't believe how beautiful he was. His thick blonde hair formed a perfect mohawk, a portent of the unique personality he'd embody as he grew. He's always marched to his own funky little beat, unafraid to be himself. When he was in fifth grade, he stood up to give a short speech at the graduation ceremony about being proud to be yourself while sporting a tee shirt that read "future fashion designer" given to him by a beloved teacher.

Then his peers began asking if he was gay. When he first came home and told me as I made dinner one night, I carefully asked, "And what did you say?"

"I told them, 'Does it matter?'," he responded, popping one of the carrots I was cutting up into his mouth as he imitated throwing his hair over his shoulder and walking off.

Unfortunately, as he entered middle school and a larger pool of classmates, the teasing would intensify. After months of bullying over his clothing and similar "gay" choices, we watched him slowly shrink into himself. He started wearing the same three plain gray tees to school, because, he said, they were the only ones he didn't get teased about. I found his favorite fashion designer tee shoved into a box at the back of his closet while cleaning one day. He pulled the edges of his personality in, valiantly trying to fit into the boxes his peers would be more comfortable with.

There's an episode of a cartoon he used to love, where the main character, a little yellow sponge named SpongeBob, tries to be more normal at the request of his neighbor, Squidward. The unique edges and holes of his little spongey self slowly disappear until finally, he's a round, totally unremarkable and generic shape and personality, ignoring the activities and style and people he truly loves as he attempts to be "normal". I watched the real-life version of this episode play out in front of me, as my son eschewed the clothing and activities he loved in an effort to be what the other kids found acceptable.

Thankfully, it didn't last. As he started eighth grade, the idea of bus life entered the scene, and he began homeschooling. Over the next few months, he slowly unpacked all the boxes he'd been trying to fit his own too muchness into, until the vibrant kid who'd stood on a platform a few years before and talked about being yourself returned to us. The lesson he learned from that experience, at such a young age, was profound; I don't believe Aidyn will ever try to put himself into a box of anyone else's making ever again.

Today, I'm not sure I've ever met anyone who belongs more to themselves. Self-possessed with a quicksilver wit, he's the one that keeps us laughing with his clever stories and lightening quick comebacks. While he didn't do exceedingly well in traditional school, his brain is a storehouse of information, and in a battle of wits he comes to the arena completely armed. He's stoic, easygoing, quick to laugh, and my number one fan, a self-professed mama's boy. I always say parenting him is like parenting an iceberg; there's so much below the surface hardly anyone ever gets to see, but as long as he's kept at the right temperature and his basic needs are met, he's content to just sit in his little corner of ocean doing his thing good naturedly.

His sister, on the other hand, is like parenting fire. Give her too much of any one thing, and she'll quickly turn into an inferno that destroys the status quo around her. Conversely, try to keep her small and contained and you'll smother the glorious spirit she possesses. When she was young, I always told people she was either going to change the world or burn it down, and that's only become more apparent as she's grown.

Her entrance into it was as animated as she's always been. A month before her caesarean was to be performed, scheduled in advance to avoid the same issues I encountered with Aidyn, I began to have problems severe enough I was admitted to the hospital to try to stabilize them. They couldn't find the root of the issues, but it appeared my body had, for reasons unknown, become unable to deal with the pregnancy and was trying to send me into premature labor. It was decided an amniocentesis, where they would extract amniotic fluid through a large needle, should be done to determine if her lungs were ready. If they were, we would move her caesarean up and take her out immediately. If they weren't, they would continue to try to keep me stable and work to stop labor for another week or so until she wouldn't need medical intervention to help her breathe.

The test revealed her lungs weren't ready. A few hours later, however, my water broke, removing any option to wait as I was rushed into the operating room. This time was much different than the first; no soft lighting and calm music playing as I was prepared, no excitement in the air. Doctors and nurses rushed around me in the cold room, neonatal staff filing in with various equipment prepared to whisk a baby whose lungs weren't ready for the world off as soon as she was born. As they began, all I could see was Evan's tense, pale face above me, the rigid set of his jaw while he waited for a glimpse of our daughter before she was taken away.

And then I heard her cry. Shrill and indignant, her loud newborn wails carried through the cold operating room and a spark of dawning registered in my petrified brain – if she's crying, she's breathing. The room erupted in cheers and sobs wracked my body as the most beautiful sound I'd ever heard, her outraged and lusty cries, continued to carry through it. Arriving right when she wanted to, defying what the world expected of her, my Ely entered the world.

I didn't get to see her for hours after. Evan went with her while she was given her first bath and they took time to make sure the problems I'd begun having were stable now I'd delivered. When she was finally placed in my arms, I refused to let her go. For almost twenty-four hours, I clutched my wee daughter to me, so much smaller than her brother had been, unable to tear my eyes away from the miracle I held. She had a head full of curly, copper-colored hair and the most perfect tiny pucker of a mouth, with bright blue eyes that seemed much too old to belong to a newborn.

She was mischievous, a little imp with the face of an angel and a penchant for trouble. When she was two, she crawled out of her crib and stole the scissors from my yarn basket, cutting off her long curls until only a few inches of hair remained, stubbornly insisting to me as I bawled over the golden locks lying on the bathroom floor, "I pwitty, mama, I pwitty!"

And she is. Gorgeous, that is, inside and out. As she aged, her empathy and awareness of the people around her would become her defining factors. She's the first to stand up for the underdog and last to tolerate injustice. She's what people call an old soul, an earthmother, holding knowledge far beyond her teenage years. When she walks into a room, she'll immediately gravitate toward the person most in need of a hug and wrap them up in one. She's also a terror in the mornings and the last person you want to get into a fight with, between her stubbornness and intellectual mind. When she gets an idea in her head, wrong or right, you never know if she'll decide to die on her chosen hill, intractable and headstrong, or suddenly relent, thoughtfully retreating while admitting she hadn't considered that point of view and she should learn more. I stand by my initial assessment – she will either change this world or burn it down. Only time will tell which she'll choose.

I'm insanely proud of my children, and who they're becoming. Neither wants to go to college, neither knows what they want to be when they grow up, and neither cares about your opinion of them, thank you very much. Both are kind and loyal, brave and strong. They'll likely finish and graduate school together this next year, a year and two, respectively, ahead of schedule. Aidyn's been talking about maybe being a teacher so he can help kids who struggled like him in school someday, and Ellery's been tossing around the idea of pursuing an apprenticeship as a tattoo artist when she's old enough.

They're both happy to have once lived and traveled on a bus, and equally happy to now wave goodbye to us when we take off to travel for a few weeks at a time. I will never stop being grateful for the events that led us into bus life and homeschooling, and the additional time and space it gave all three of us to truly know our children and share so much we might have otherwise missed with them. When they graduate, I'm absolutely looking forward to being able to spend more time traveling as my mom duties lessen and their own lives as adults begin. But these two humans I've birthed and raised and loved and learned from and laughed with and been humbled by — they are the greatest adventure of my lifetime.

The Island of the Gods

I went snorkeling for the first time in my life, after learning how to swim the same week.

If you saw that post, you know I did it for my fish of a husband, who is the most beautiful thing I've ever seen in the water. I'm less a fish and more a frantic looking octopus. But I knew he wanted to go, and I was determined not to be that wife that stays on the boat or holds him back.

As I sat on the edge of the traditional-style Balinese boat, watching everyone else dive off into the ocean, paralyzing fear gripped me.

What if I drown? What if there's a shark? What if my swimsuit falls off? What if water goes into my snorkel and I can't breathe, and no one notices, and I slowly die in my mask?

And then a bigger fear gripped me. What if I don't do this, and I regret it for the rest of my life?

I looked at Mike - and I jumped in.

The ocean swallowed me momentarily, and then I got my bearings and bobbed up. It was a little panic inducing learning how to breathe through the snorkel, but I suddenly realized I was doing it.

And I was loving it.

My swimsuit did actually fall off a little when a wave caught me. We did actually see a shark. And I did get a face full of water in my snorkel and mask, although I didn't drown slowly.

I also watched my husband free dive and explore the caves beneath us, smiling proudly when the others in our party paddled over to ask me if he was a professional of some sort as he swam to startling depths to explore the sea floor below us. I played with fish. I saw things many people only see in pictures. I loved every minute of it.

And I swam in the freaking ocean friends.

There's only one fear you should allow in your life, and that's what happens if you don't take the risks that frighten you.

There is so much unlived life waiting on the other side of them.

(October 16, 2019)

They call it the Island of the Gods, and it's easy to believe at least one must reside among the turquoise waters and towering coconut trees. For me, it will forever be the place I shed the last of my inhibitions, where I started saying yes to everything instead of maybe. And that may sound strange to admit, as we'd already upturned our lives to turn a school bus into a tiny home and, for all intents and purposes, appeared to say yes to our dreams more often than not. But I still had a fair share of inhibitions holding me back from living fully, pieces of myself I didn't embrace or acknowledge, fears that caused me to shrink. I started to write that Bali released me from those shackles, but that isn't exactly true. Bali just gave me reasons to move beyond them.

It started the day we arrived, after thirty hours of travel. As the sun set on the tropical island that would be our home for the next month, and we made our way to the villa we'd rented, I'd be given my first opportunity to conquer my fears and say yes. The driver we'd hired to drive us the two hours from the airport to our Airbnb, Yoga, finally turned off the main road and into a small parking lot. Just enough light remained to see the winding lane leading away from it, what I thought was a sidewalk at first. Waiting in the lot was our host, Kadek, sitting on a silver scooter. After introducing himself, he talked quickly to Yoga, who got back into his small car and pulled it around into a parking space. Kadek said he'd need to take our bags to the villa, and suddenly, all our luggage was disappearing into the quickly darkening night down the path I suddenly realized wasn't a sidewalk at all, but a road.

Yoga suddenly reappeared on a red scooter, a wide smile on his face as he explained he would help Kadek take us to our temporary home. I didn't have time to properly register what this meant before the man in question zoomed back out of the night, sans luggage, and held out a helmet to me. I turned to see Mike climbing onto the red scooter behind Yoga, and it dawned on me I was supposed to do the same with Kadek.

"We can't walk?" I asked.

"It's a long walk," Kadek said encouragingly. "I take you."

I strapped the helmet on my head and clambered on behind him. I had just enough time to catch a glimpse of Mike, comically huge behind Yoga, before Kadek gunned it and we roared off into the night. The scooter turned this way and that, down what appeared to be ever narrowing lanes, barely slowing the breakneck pace he'd set as we veered right and left. I had a vague impression of buildings and walls and looming trees, but between the speed and now complete darkness, it was hard to tell what we were passing. My arms were locked around his waist in what I'm sure was a crushing grip, and I think I would have been screaming in terror if I had been able to breathe.

And then the almost full moon broke through the night as we rounded another corner, opening up the landscape around us. We were racing down the narrowest of concrete paths, barely wide enough for the scooter we rode, beside rice fields waving in the slight breeze. In the distance I could see the looming silhouette of the jungle meeting the fields, dotted with walled villas and restaurants spaced along the haphazard road. It suddenly occurred to me that while my family and friends were waking up to go about their daily lives, half a world away, I was racing on a scooter through a rice field in the middle of a mild Balinese night. My grip loosened, my sudden peals of laughter lost to the wind whipping by us. Kadek laughed with me as we wound a final turn, and suddenly, we were in front of a large iron gate in the high plaster wall.

He led us through the gate and a short courtyard into the garden, where an infinity pool glowed amid the trees and vines. Beyond it lay our villa, lit up against the night. Only the large bedroom, with its draped four poster bed, was completely indoors behind glass walls. The kitchen, living space, and bathroom were designed in such a way they simply melted into the outdoors, including the huge stone bathtub and shower built among the rocks of the exterior wall. As our hosts bid us good evening and Mike slid the heavy bolt shut on the gate, I wandered through the house and back into the garden to step up onto the edge of the pool in my bare feet, the cool water running over the side into the rocks below. Clusters of frangipani flowers hung within my reach, the air heavy with their sweet scent, and one appeared in front of me as Mike noiselessly walked up behind me to pluck one and wrap me up in his arms while setting it in my hand, his lips on my neck as he whispered, "Welcome home."

He pulled away, and I turned in time to see his clothes fall to the ground. He dove into the pool, his naked body gleaming in the moonlight, and resurfaced with a crooked grin beckoning me to join him. Normally, I would have smiled and shrugged, letting my exhaustion or insecurities or any myriad of other excuses interrupt the magic of the moment. But, still on the heady high of the scooter ride, I instead let my dress slip from shoulders and walked, freer than I'd ever felt in my life, down the shallow stairs into the sparkling water as he watched. The air was sweet and heavy, his body against mine in the humid night, another adventure begun.

Now before I spout any more poetic nonsense about Bali, I will tell you – in some ways, it's not all it's cracked up to be. Tourism has, in some ways, been a detriment there, as once unique experiences were canned and recreated across the whole of the island for Instagram moments and sacred places crammed full of people. We wanted to see a specific temple, and Kadek told us we'd want to go early before the crowds came. We left in the wee hours of the morning to drive several hours and get there as it opened, only to find it already completely packed with people entering the gates. As we were shuffled through, we were told to take a ticket to await our turn, numbered 97. We assumed this meant our turn into the temple, but we quickly discovered as we milled around it was the line to have your photo taken in front of the large gates overlooking the volcano beyond them. A small group of Balinese men were stationed in front of them; as your number was called, you'd hand them your camera and go stand in the gates, where they would yell "next pose" over and over while taking photos, holding a mirror under the phone in such a way it appeared you were on the edge of a massive pool of water instead of a large courtyard filled with hundreds of other people.

Behind this, on the massive stairways leading up to the smaller gates that went into the inner parts of the temple tourists were barred from, lines formed in front of each to have your photo taken there as well. It was part of the experience we'd get used to, standing in line to capture your own magical Bali photo at well-known locations, but in this moment, it was a bit of a shock to be confronted with all this hubbub before we'd even had breakfast. Our guide for the day, also named Kadek, purchased us small cups of black coffee and banana rice balls wrapped in leaves, and we watched the chaos around us as we ate our simple breakfast and discussed if we really wanted to wait just to get a photo as they called the next number, 32. This

Kadek didn't speak English as well as the first, but we managed to communicate that we weren't looking for this experience and didn't care about the photos so much as seeing the architecture and learning the history. He nodded, suddenly animated, and with a smile crowed, "I know, I know, come!", rushing off back the way we'd come and away from the growing crowd.

He led us back down the mountain and entered a smaller side gate. Looking back up, we could see we were now in the courtyard at the bottom of the large gates, where above us people were still doing their yoga and jumping poses between them. Not as grand as the one above, this courtyard had no high walls but opened directly out the side the mountain, the volcano seemingly closer here and valley spread out below it clearly visible. The only others here were the Balinese people making their pilgrimages, dressed in temple clothes as they climbed the steps beyond us with baskets perched on their heads. We sat and watched them pass, enjoying the silence after the crush of people, snapping photos of the intricately carved stone and panorama views.

But that's not what I remember about Bali, not really. It would take me another book entirely to explain what we learned and experienced in one month on that island. The culture and people, the intricacies of their way of life, the beauty of their beliefs and artwork that springs readily from their capable hands. We fell completely in love with the people and island while we temporarily resided there, making friendships we continue long distance to this day. But alas, I have only one chapter in this book about a bus to explain the biggest lesson I learned there, the seeming culmination of all the ones bus life has given me, so let's return to that.

A few weeks after that first midnight swim, a habit that became routine for us while we were there, our time was winding down. We'd traversed the island and enjoyed the sights and food and experiences, but there were still two Mike wanted to have. And neither were high up on my to do list if I was honest.

Most intimidating of these was snorkeling in the ocean. My husband is a fish in water, sleek and powerful and agile. Already equipped with a certain proclivity to it, his time training in and for the military programs he was involved in had honed his swimming and diving skills until he was as comfortable under the water as on land. He used to amuse himself at the pool near our house by letting me tie his hands and feet up before he'd jump into the deep end, and I'd watch apprehensively as he'd sit calmly at the bottom untying himself. He'd always resurface after a few minutes to throw the ropes and a grin my way before striking out to do endless rounds of laps. I watched all this from the side, because unlike my confident husband, I didn't know how to swim.

As a child I didn't have the opportunity, and by the time I was an adult, I was actually slightly terrified of the water and never wanted to learn. Which meant when he said he wanted to go snorkeling in the ocean, *the ocean*, panic immediately gripped me. Looking at my face, he backpedaled and shrugged it off, telling me it wasn't a big deal. Relief flooded me. And then shame. Hot, overwhelming waves of it. I could see the desire in his eyes as he continued to scan the website of activities we'd been looking at, feel the absolute longing radiating from him as he looked at pictures of clear waters filled with turtles and fish. The water is home to him in a way I don't understand, but as he always does, he prepared to stay abroad from it for my sake. And suddenly, the only thing more terrifying to me than jumping into the great wide ocean was keeping him away from it.

"You could teach me," I blurted out.

"What, teach you to swim?" he asked, surprised. I'd always turned down his offers before, content to watch him enjoy the water from the sidelines.

"Yeah, here in our pool. You could teach me, and we can go at the end of the week after I learn."

Excitement flushed his face, and before I knew it, he was in the pool, water droplets dripping from his hair over the huge smile on his face while he waited for me. I approached the pool much as I imagine I would the guillotine. "So this is how I die," I muttered to myself.

Between our trips to the market and temples, in every moment of free time, he taught me how to swim. We purchased a small snorkel and mask for me so he could teach me how to effectively use and clear it, and every day I dutifully climbed into the pool with it strapped to my face, ready for more torture. I was less a fish in water, and more, as I wrote on our Instagram post, a frantic looking octopus flailing madly around him. But day by day, little by little, I got more and more comfortable in the water and with the mask, able to keep myself afloat and, at the very least, not feel like I was seconds from drowning every time I was in deeper water.

The day of our expedition dawned bright and clear, and Mike nearly ran to the car waiting to take us. His infectious energy spilled over, and I found myself actually looking forward to our excursion. We found our boat and climbed aboard with the handful of people from around the globe who'd also booked snorkeling as their day's tourist attraction. It was a beautiful one, and the water was exactly as the photos depicted it, clear and turquoise and teeming with life. We all chatted as the boat sped toward the first cove we'd be stopping at, and it wasn't until the engine died away my fear returned. Pulling on my flippers and mask, I watched the others somersault and dive off the side of the wood boat, trying to ignore the rising panic tightening my chest. Then I saw Mike, treading water, his smile bright and happy under the mask, waiting for me. I might not be at home in the water, but mine was there waiting for me in it, I realized, safe and secure as always. I took a breath and dived in.

What followed was magic. Pure, unadulterated, unbound, wild magic. The way the ocean held me as I swayed on the surface, the schools of fish that swam right up to my mask and surrounded me, watching Mike dive to the floor where coral cities teemed with life and bigger fish like sharks and grouper lurked. Every hour or so we'd climb back up onto the boat and take off for a new piece of ocean, stopping at each to appreciate the unique sights they offered, until I no longer paused before diving off the side and into the depths. At the final stop of the day, I told Mike I was tired and would stay on the boat this time along with a woman who'd gotten a little seasick. I'd noticed he was limiting himself, determined to stay beside me and make sure I was okay as I faced my fears, and I'd decided it was time to hold myself back now to allow him space to fully enjoy this last dive.

I watched from the boat, chatting with the woman beside

me as he dove over and over into these deeper and choppier waters. He remained in them as the others started straggling in and climbing aboard, enjoying every remaining second he could. The man whose wife I'd stayed behind with came over as he toweled off to check on her, and he gestured to Mike, who'd finally started swimming back with long, powerful strokes. "Is that your husband?"

I nodded, watching him quickly approach.

"Man, I've never seen anything like that. Is he a professional diver or something? He went all the way down, must have been forty feet, to where the turtles were cruising on the floor," he exclaimed. "He just stayed down there, for like, ever. We were all just watching him instead of the turtles!"

"He did some diving in the military," I answered, as the subject of his awe broke the surface of the waves and heaved himself in one fluid motion out of them. "He just really loves the water."

"I'll say," he laughed, walking over to tell Mike himself how impressed he was. We ate an early dinner with them beside the incoming surf when we returned to shore, reliving the events of the day, and then returned to our villa, where Mike's first move was to return to the pool. This time, I didn't need an invitation to join him. The water still wasn't my home, but I was no longer a tourist there either.

His other big wish wasn't as hard for me to acquiesce to, as it involved a sunrise; I can be bribed into almost any activity if it involves the rising or setting sun. He wanted to climb Mount Batur to watch the sunrise over Mount Agung beyond it. In order to this we would leave our villa at one in the morning, drive a couple of hours, and climb one active volcano in the dark to be in place at the right time to witness the sun come up over the other one in the distance. It wasn't the early rising or dark or active volcano part that scared me. It was the four-and-a-half-mile trek up the side of a mountain.

See, I'd stopped working out when we left the gym. Tired to my bones, mentally and physically, from a decade of nonstop workouts and hustle mentality, I'd traded weights for my yoga mat and taken a conscious break from training. I wasn't in bad shape, by any means, but after not working out for a year in any real way, the idea of trying to drag myself up a mountain, keeping up with Mike, was intimidating. Only my extreme love of sunrises propelled me to book the excursion and pull out my sneakers for the first time on the trip. Mike didn't notice any apprehension from me, taking my fitness level for granted I suppose, and I decided not to discuss it with him.

As if the Universe was determined to push me as far outside my comfort zone as possible, we were paired with another young American couple who spent most of their time traveling around hiking and passed the drive up talking about how jazzed they were to make the climb. Our guide was a young guy quickly overcome with my companions' excited energy, who translated it as our group of four wanting to get up the mountain as quickly as possible. When I tell you we set off from the base camp of the trailhead at a run, I mean a literal run. Before I knew what was happening, not only was I climbing a mountain in the dark wee hours of the morning, I was jogging my way up it, dodging roots and rocks in the path, passing the other early morning hikers slowly enjoying their way up the small trail. Our guide veered off the path at times, forging his own as we dodged larger groups of more moderately paced climbers and yelling, "Faster, faster, yes?"

It's funny. My brain kept repeating, "You can't do this, you can't do this", even as I ran. It wasn't until we'd gotten halfway up the volcano and paused at the small camp there where outhouses had been built I actually realized I was, in fact, doing it. We barely stopped and then we were running again, sprinting toward the final stretch where it turned to hand over feet climbing. At this point, I experienced altitude sickness from the quick change in it for the first time in my life. The world started swimming before my eyes and I had a moment of fear I was going to collapse at the last moment after all that pushing, but the little Balinese woman who was our guide's assistant grabbed my hand and literally towed me over the remaining several hundred feet to the precipice of the caldera, where she plunked me down on a rock and went off to gather breakfast. Mike and our new friends laughed as our guide told us we'd just set a record for his quickest trip up in four years while he sat making me sip water, and slowly the world came back into focus.

We ate our breakfast on the rim of the volcano, chocolate bars and bananas and hot Balinese coffee and hardboiled eggs cooked in the thermally heated stream there. The first sliver of light appeared in the distance, and I held my husband's hand as one of the most beautiful sunrises I'd ever seen appeared over the rim of the neighboring volcano in the distance. I have a photo of that morning framed, Mike and I silhouetted against the sunrise on the edge of a smoking volcano. The monkeys that live on the ridge had just stolen what was left of my banana, and there's laughter lingering on our faces.

"Run down, fastest down too?" our guide prompted, as we turned to leave in the bright morning light.

"Yes," I answered. "Run down too."

I came home from Bali changed, different. I hadn't realized how much fear still held me back, even after entering bus life, and how often I still said no as a result. But that's the beauty of travel, isn't it? It changes you, heals you, teaches you, uncovers parts of yourself you didn't know existed, and turns you into a storyteller. I think I fall in love a little with every place I visit and leave a little part of myself there when we leave. I used to hate that moment, the parting, the going home. But this time, as we packed up to leave this little piece of heaven on earth, I wasn't dreading it the way I normally did.

Don't get me wrong – I was going to miss the constant smell of frangipani flowers, the old rice farmer on the corner who yelled, "selamat pagi!" to us every morning as we passed, and the fresh fruit we bought for breakfast each day. But this time, we were coming home to Oliver, and the proverbial life we'd created we didn't need a vacation from. And I didn't need my Bali lesson to say an emphatic yes to that.

Into the Sunset

Me: "But what if we fall in love with every place we go, and we can never pick just one to settle in?"

Him: "Then what a beautiful life we'll lead, always in love."

(October 7, 2019)

I've lost track of how many miles have rolled under our tires and the number of spots we've pulled off into and made home for the night. So too how many feet of airport terminals my favorite boots have walked and the number of cities they've explored with me. Such is the life of a nomad. But this I do know. From the time I was young, my happiest moments involved a plane ticket and passport in my hand, and I knew I would spend my life traveling.

I have a good friend who has little desire to travel anywhere else. Her roots spread wide and deep in the Montana soil, and she loves the safety and security of knowing exactly where home is. And that's beautiful, in its own way. To belong so deeply to a place it always calls you back. To be still and allow life to meet you where you stand.

That's not my story. My home has wheels, and my heart has wings. Both have to move fairly often, or they start to rust. The truth is, there's only one thing in the world that brings me absolute and unequivocal joy, and that's a new horizon looming. Even when it's hard, even when it goes completely upside down, travel will always be my purest love. As the saying goes, I'd rather die on an adventure than live standing still.

But the single greatest lesson bus life has given me is that adventure isn't just found on the road. It exists everywhere, in almost every facet of our everyday lives. We converted a school bus and drove all over the wilds to find the greatest adventure we'd share was this bigger journey we call life, with all its seemingly boring in-between moments. Exploring foreign underwater landscapes, climbing mountains to see the view from the top, traipsing through foreign countries, watching a billion stars light up the velvet darkness – nothing can compare to the exquisite adventure that is our short existence on this planet, and what we choose to do with our time here, however big or small. I am so grateful for each and every one of the moments I've been privileged to experience, but a list of my favorites might surprise you.

Words whispered in my ear in the dark of night as I drift

off to sleep, my teenage daughter curled up under my arm as she tells me she hopes she has my courage when she's older, the smile Evan gives me where his eyes crinkle up, reminding me that while our marriage might not have worked, our roots run so deep we weathered the storm, and the first time my son wrapped me up in his arms while I cried and I realized it was a young man that held me, no longer a boy. In other words, in the same way that home is no single spot on a map for me, adventure isn't a route along it either. Every day is an adventure, if we simply decide to find the thrills hidden in the seemingly mundane.

Not to say all adventures are created equal, or that I will ever stop loving to travel. I hope the feel of that plane ticket in my hand still thrills me just as much when I'm ninety as it does now, but there's a peace in me, a contentedness to simply be, that I didn't possess before I lived in a bus.

Out of all the lessons bus life has passed my way, this is the one I'm most grateful for. I used to simply exist between adventures, passing the time in the middle impatiently as an inconvenience that must be dealt with. It saddens me to think how much of my life I wasted on this mentality, how many adventures I missed because I had such a narrow view of what one was. Bus life gave me that gift, the broadening of my mind and definitions to realize how many small adventures life gives us each and every day. Sitting in the driver's seat of a school bus also put me in the driver's seat of my own life, in many ways, and I don't think I will ever sit in the passenger's seat, allowing the scenery to drift by, again.

A follower on Instagram recently responded to a story of mine. "Is there anything you can't do and aren't good at?! You just seem to have it all figured out. Everything you do looks like magic. I doubt I will ever have even a small part of what you make look effortless figured out. Keep sharing, it's inspiring to us mortals."

Obviously, I laughed. And also, (maybe not so) obviously, I don't, have it all figured out that is. No one does after all. And that's as it should be. How absolutely mundane life would be if there was nothing left to learn, no hurdles or barriers to cross. While I've sometimes wished life was smoother sailing during the storms I've weathered, I've never regretted the navigational skills I learned as we maneuvered through them or the rainbow moments that followed when the clouds parted. Sometimes, during those seasons of cloudless blue skies and beautiful sunshine, I start to think I do have it all figured out. And every time, as if on cue, the clouds start to build on the horizon as a new storm with lessons all its own brews.

I chuckled when I responded, assuring her it wasn't true. In fact, I told her, the night before she'd messaged, I'd gone to bed upset because I'd lain there ruminating about a scenario until I was thoroughly disgruntled. The kicker? It was entirely made up in my mind. I'd literally created a fear-based projection in my head of what *could* happen and allowed it to fill my head with waking nightmares until I was legitimately on the verge of tears about this completely imaginary story line. Does this, I concluded, sound like a woman who has it all figured out?

I'm a classic overthinker, sometimes about plot lines that don't actually exist. I'm demanding, both of myself and others, and there are times when my impatience startles even me with the severity of its expectations. I'm a back seat driver, can be selfish and manipulative if I'm not careful while in a fear or anger-based emotional state, and I think far too highly of my own opinion, to the detriment of considering others might have one to share.

Social media doesn't show these underlying currents of personality, of course. They just see a curly haired woman laughing at the camera. In one shot she weaves a blanket on a loom while a pie cools in the window and a garden overflows with produce of every color beyond it. In another she stands highlighted with a school bus against a shocking sunset in the desert or beside the rolling waves of the ocean. But behind the scenes, just out of view, never forget the flurry of wild activity that accompanies every person's life production, the blooper reel of unflattering moments where it all went awry.

That's not to say I don't have at least a few things figured out after my own personal storms, at least up to my current points of understanding and reference. And I think that's how this book is supposed to end, with the lessons I've learned while living the tales in its pages. So here goes.

You're the only one who has to live your story. You. Not your parents, not your friends, and definitely not the strangers giving you flack on social media. And if they don't have to live it, and feel it, and deal with its outcomes, perhaps you should care less about their perceptions and thoughts about it and do it in a way that makes you feel more alive. You are not obligated to make sense to anyone, and as long as you're keeping your side of the street clean, live a life that makes sense to you, and more than that, makes you feel alive.

Edit your life. Be absolutely savage about it, callous even, like you're downsizing from a three-story house to live in a school bus. And if you ever find, while editing, a certain section no longer makes sense or pertains to the subject matter, delete it and rewrite a new chapter that does. A blank new page is scary, but you know what's scarier? Reading a book at the end of your life telling a story you didn't actively write and doesn't sound like you. If you're not holding the pen to the pages of your own, trust that someone else will pick it up and do all that writing for you, and the finished book might not be one you care to read.

Start where you are, right now, with what you have. It's easy to make excuses for why our lives don't look the way we want them to, and much harder to fight uphill for our dreams. But as someone who's stood on the top of a few hills I clawed my way to the top of, let me let you in on a little secret. Those moments in my life, standing there, bruised and battered and dirty and looking down at how far I'd come was worth every second I spent hauling myself up. I can't tell you how many people have asked us how we did it, and then started telling me all the reasons they can't. And you know what? They're right. Because we believe what we tell ourselves.

I won't say no matter where you are or what the circumstances, you can change your life, because that's a vast oversimplification. There are many hurdles that take a lot more than a can-do attitude to jump. But I'd wager in many situations, if you quit waiting for an ideal one and simply grabbed onto the present one with both hands and refused to let go, you'd find there's a lot you can do with what you have to start taking steps up that hill. You want to become a master gardener? Start with a small pot on a window ledge. You want to be a world traveler? Cut expenses where you're being frivolous to start saving for a trip, even if it's just a few dollars a week, then download an app to start learning the language in the meantime. You want to turn a school bus into a tiny home? Start downsizing and selling off what you won't be able to take with you to start a school bus fund for yourself and declutter your life in the meantime. In other words, if you have a dream, don't wait for the perfect time to chase it. Even if you're taking baby steps, start moving forward however you can right now.

You don't, and never should, have it completely figured out. And that's okay. If you're doing the best you can with what you have, where you're at, you're doing it right. All we can do, any of us, is to try. And hopefully make the lives of people around us and the world better along the way. It doesn't need more people living lives deemed successful by outdated and rigid thought processes. It needs people trying their best, telling their stories. People willing to fight for their own happiness and that of others. Courageous souls unafraid to redefine what success truly looks like while living a life that makes them feel they're actually alive, following their hearts even when no one else can understand the rhythm it beats to.

Have the courage to admit when you're wrong. We all are from time to time, after all, and one of the most validating gifts we can give to others is to tell them when we've realized we made a mistake instead of trying to cover it over. It takes a lot of bravery to humbly admit, with no qualifications or excuses, that we recognize and accept when we've been in error, and none at all to continue to bluster away and double down instead of owning up to our own moments of idiocy.

And finally, tell your story; it gives others a place to start to do the same. It doesn't matter what the pages hold. They could be filled with far-flung destinations and witty anecdotes, work and parenting, trials and tragedy or inspiration and hope. Whatever the tale, when we share it, we touch others living a similar one or aspiring to create a narrative like it. It surprised me, when I started living my life as an open book on social media, how many people wanted to read it. And how many people began a new chapter in their own biography because I and others telling their stories showed them how beautiful it could be to turn a page and write a different one for themselves.

As a reader, I often find myself receiving insight into the author as I devour their words. And as I wrote this, I sometimes wondered what pieces of myself readers would find tucked in these pages, what parts of my desires and hopes and dreams and regrets they would discover hidden among my words. When I was in school, a teacher once asked us, "If you could be remembered for one thing, what would it be?".

Of course, I was young and didn't have the knowledge and

experience I do now. I probably answered something from my ten-year-old ego about discovering the cure for cancer or winning a Nobel prize. But now, at this very moment, my slightly humbler thirty-six-year-old self will give an answer mirroring what I hope you discovered in the words on these pages.

Grace is the answer to both. Grace and love and gratitude. That's what I hope those I have touched remember about me, that I was graceful in my thoughts and actions. That I valued love above all else. That I was grateful even through times of despair and seeming drought.

And I hope that's also what seeps out of these pages, the parts of myself I've inadvertently woven through these words and this rambling tale that begins and ends in a school bus while traveling everywhere else in between. I didn't realize I was writing a love story until the end, but I hope you realized it sooner, because the words were knit together with it. Now finished, as I look back on them, it's what I see – a woman in love with life, her family, a school bus, travel, and a chocolate-eyed man. That man would disagree. He would contend as the words were mine, it was always going to be a love story, because that's all I know how to write. I'm not sure about that, but one thing I do know.

I think I started writing this book years ago in my head.

Even before a bus and a gym and travels, I knew I was living a story I'd want to tell someday. And now I have. But the most brilliant part, as I close out this chapter, and with it, this volume, is another waits to be written. The next part of this tale is about to unfold, and as I type these closing lines, I realize with gratitude I stand on the precipice of yet another new adventure. Maybe there will be plane tickets and travel guides and a new language to learn. Perhaps it's simply to our backyard, where the garden is in full swing and I can walk among the vines and leaves. Whatever words are about to be written on that blank page of tomorrow, all I can say for certain is that every single one of them will be absolutely and entirely mine, because a big white bus named Oliver put me in the driver's seat of my own life, and I'll never watch life pass me by from the passenger's side again.

Brass Tacks

I tried so hard to make sure I included every single question we're commonly asked here in this FAQ section. Over and over, I scoured the comments and DMs of our social media looking for every single request I could find, even going so far as to ask repeatedly in my stories to make sure there was nothing I missed.

With that said, I'm absolutely sure I missed something, because that's just the way it works. If there is a question I've failed to answer here, please know you can ask it and receive a ready answer on our social media. I would include our handle for reference, but really that just seems superfluous at this point.

What kind of bus is Oliver, and how big is he?

Oliver is an International rear engine, flat nose school bus. He was capable of holding eighty-four passengers during his working days and is forty feet long and eight feet wide.

What kind of engine and transmission do you have?

Oliver's drive train was the main reason we chose him. With a DT466 engine and Alison 3000 transmission, it's a combo that provides enough power to keep us going strong even on hills and is easy and affordable to work on in the event it has an issue.

What is your gas mileage like?

Oliver averages eight to ten mile to the gallon, and has a hundred-gallon tank, meaning we can go 800 to 1,000 miles on a full tank of diesel. We get our best gas mileage on state highways, where we can cruise at around sixty. Interstates and hills cause us to dip to the lower number.

How much does Oliver weigh?

With tanks fully loaded, Oliver weighs in at 18,500 pounds, while his GVWR is 36,350 pounds. Compared to many other skoolies, Oly is pretty light!

How fast can you drive, is he slow?

Thanks to that aforementioned holy grail of drive trains and lighter build weight, Oliver is pretty zippy. Many of our friends in the skoolie community do have buses that top out at a certain speed and aren't as peppy, but Oliver isn't among them.

Once while jamming out to road tunes and enjoying a long stretch of smooth interstate, I looked down at my speedometer to see we were barreling down the road at eighty-five miles per hour! My happy cruising speed is generally around seventy. Even on hills he does pretty well, rarely going below forty. There was once a very long uphill grade outside of Las Vegas that took us down to twenty-five by the time we hit the top, but that's more the exception than the rule.

Did you have trouble getting the bus registered?

We didn't, but the hoops you have to jump through vary state to state. Oliver is registered as a Class A motorhome. In order to achieve his changed status from kid hauler to tiny home, we were required to have a sheriff come walk through and check off that we had certain systems in place, including a self-contained toilet, cooking apparatus, and sleeping space.

Do you need a CDL to drive?

Again, this varies state to state, but in ours, no. Once the seats were removed, a special license was no longer required. It all simply depends on the state you choose to register in.

Do you have trouble parking in RV parks?

We haven't, personally. However, we took pains to make Oliver blend in, as much as a forty-foot school bus with a stove pipe sticking out the top can anyway. Because he's a neutral color and very clean looking from the outside, we've never been turned away from an RV park. However, we've also only parked at one in the almost three years we've been doing this, so it's hard to say if we would have experienced more issues had we tried to utilize parks more.

Have you ever been told to move in the middle of the night?

We haven't. Again, this is probably just good odds. We don't chance parking in places with no parking signs or that might be private property, ask permission to stay if we suspect it might be an issue, and mostly park on public lands that allow wild camping.

What are the technical details of the build – water, solar, etc.?

We have one hundred-gallon water tank under our bed, two forty-gallon water tanks in our under storage, two five-gallon propane tanks, six hundred watts of solar panels, and six hundred amp hours of lithium batteries.

What are your bathroom walls made of?

We used a product called Ardex feather finish concrete to create the walls and floor of our bathroom, as well as our kitchen counters and wood stove surround. While it looks like heavy poured concrete, it's just a veneer finish that's incredibly lightweight. To give you some perspective, we used about ten bags for the whole bus, each weighing ten pounds, for a total of 100 pounds of concrete for both the bathroom and kitchen. The forms are made from wood and sealed with a special rubber paint to keep them waterproof. The concrete is laid on in a few thin layers, then sealed with a food grade waterproof sealer to make them nonporous. They've held up beautifully during our travels, with a few hairline cracks appearing but nothing that's required heavy repairs

If you could do your build over again, what would you change?

We've actually already remodeled most of the components we found we didn't like after living here for a while and learning what worked and what didn't. This included removing our combo washer/dryer unit to replace it with a bathtub, changing out the kids' bunk beds for dual couches (one of which was murphy-style and could fold up into the wall), and then changing those dual couches out again when the kids stopped traveling with us to put in a real couch and more extensive bookshelf system. This year we added further water storage to the bus, and in the process reworked our original bed design to include storage bins instead of large drawers. Aside from these already completed changes, I can't honestly say there's a single thing I'd change if we could do it over.

Was it hard to adjust to bus life?

There were, of course, elements of bus life we had to get used to. Filling the water tanks, for instance, wasn't a chore we were used to. But living tiny wasn't a huge adjustment, either because we were so ready for this new adventure we just didn't notice or because we'd already pared down our belongings to so few and were already somewhat used to it. I remember I expected to not to be able to sleep that first night in the bus, with all the sounds around us, and woke up surprised the next day when I opened my eyes to the sun creeping in after a peaceful night's rest. Learning to live closely to each other, without individual rooms to retreat to, was likely the biggest adjustment.

What states have you traveled to in the bus?

Over the last two years, we've explored the western half of the United States, including Washington, Oregon, California, Arizona, Nevada, Utah, New Mexico, Colorado, Wyoming, Idaho, and Montana. We'd planned to head into Canada last year, but at the time of writing, the border has only just reopened. When we started bus life, we wanted to check off every state and planned to scurry through them all, but then we learned we prefer to pick a state and trundle around it, exploring it fully and seeing many parts of it as opposed to waving at them as we pass in a hurry to the next one. Someday we will head east, I'm sure, but for now, we've thoroughly enjoyed the west.

How do you find places to stay and park?

We rely on several apps, local advice, and Google to help us find parking. Our favorite apps include Boondocking, iOverlander, and FreeRoam. All three use recommendations, reviews, and photos from other nomads and include useful information like road info, the size of rig the spot allows, and whether internet is available. Sometimes while stopping in to fill up our tanks, locals will mention spots we can check out and park at. And sometimes, we just pull up a Google map and do some scouting for the nearest Wal-Mart, especially if we're just looking for a place to pull off and spend a night before moving on to a chosen destination.

Is it hard to cook in the bus?

Not at all. My kitchen on this bus is actually my favorite – it's tiny but mighty! I have plenty of counter space, an almost full-sized fridge, three burner range, and easily accessed pantry. While the oven is small, it's enough to cook a large loaf of sourdough. The main issue is making sure we pop the top hatch to allow any steam to escape.

Do you decorate your bus differently for each season still?

I do! I always liked to change décor as the mood hit in our old home, and that habit hasn't changed living tiny. Of course, now that I don't have a basement or garage to store holiday decorating items in, it looks different. Where before I would have bins of seasonal decorations stored away, now I repurpose and reuse the same objects for each season and use a lot of natural elements that can be added to our compost heap instead of stored away. For instance, during the Halloween/Samhain season, I decorated with pumpkins and cornstalks from our garden. For Christmas/Yule, we used juniper boughs and dried oranges and cranberry garlands. During the summer, I bring in lots of live plants in pots.

What causes you anxiety when, after all, you are living a life full of incredible moments?

I will first just say that anxiety and depression don't discriminate. They aren't the result of bad life circumstances, and they aren't cured by a perfect life. Some of the most blessed people I've known, in terms of their life circumstances, have also dealt with some of the biggest mental health hurdles, while others in what appear to be terrible circumstances are able to coast through life with a much sunnier outlook. Our life is blessed, of this I am aware and profoundly grateful. But I've struggled with anxiety and depression my entire life, and the bus didn't change that hormonal roller coaster. It did give me more space to deal with it somewhat more gracefully, but the same thoughts that caused anxiety before (money, my kids, relationships, work problems) still exist. Bus life is absolutely full of incredible moments, one I will be forever grateful I have been able to experience. But it isn't removed from all life's worries and woes, and even comes with a few of its own. In other words, bus life is full of happy times, but it isn't a cure all for anxiety and depression.

How do you winterize the bus?

We've spent at least part of two Montana winters in this bus, and even in temperatures down to -25 degrees, we've been able to live mostly comfortably and without too much hassle in this little bus. Our wood stove provides us with plenty of heat, but we take additional steps as well. Our pipes are insulated, and we have a small diesel heater we can run if necessary on the coldest days. We add plastic to our windows, creating a greenhouse effect that traps in sunlight and keeps drafts at bay. Our front window panels keep heat from escaping through those big front windows, and we add an insulated curtain to the door for the same reason. Finally, we use supplemental heating sources like electric blankets to keep the chill at bay.

How do you make money on the road?

This is the single biggest question we're asked, understandably, as so many people are wanting to break away from the nine to five and be freer to live a life untethered from the traditional job model. Mike and I both started road life creating SEO content for a company called The HOTH. Essentially, we write content for businesses designed to increase their rankings in web searches, increasing their visibility online. As time passed, our social media grew to such a point that it became more and more my full-time job, as well as providing me with additional opportunities like running the social media platforms of other companies. Today, Mike's full-time job is the same he started with, writing SEO content for companies. Mine is a little more varied, with our social media platforms and website now demanding most of my time and making up a good portion of our income. To preemptively answer the next question we're asked, that income is made up through a mix of brand deals, affiliate kickbacks for products we use and endorse, and selling our own goods and services.

What are your average expenses?

It really just depends on the month. When we're parked at home base, we have only a handful of expenses – namely our phone/internet, groceries, insurance, and propane if it needs to be filled. When we travel, we add diesel to that list. If we're paying to park or experience attractions along the way or have a repair or maintenance bill pop up, that obviously adds to it.

What maintenance is required on the bus?

Fluid and filter changes are the most common. Beyond that, there's air system checks and tank monitoring, cleaning the wood stove out, refilling propane and water, and various random chores that pop up from time to time like blowing out the engine compartment and giving him a good wash.

What do you do for internet?

We used a Verizon MiFi for a long time, but are currently switching over to a more in-depth system that's essentially another phone line in a router to give us better access with no throttled speeds. Because suddenly hitting your megabyte usage and waiting for the show you're trying to binge watch buffer isn't a good time.

Do you have to deal with any local bylaws that prohibit tiny living?

We've been fortunate not to experience this where we park, but it's a common concern in tiny home circles. We always recommend you check in the area you plan to build and reside in to ensure it's compatible before buying a bus and then finding out your plans aren't allowed. Many neighborhoods have covenants with very specific language. When traveling and parking, you'll want to watch to make sure there's no posted signage prohibiting parking. In many cases, it fully depends on other people's reactions. We know people parked on land that has a strict "no living in RVs" verbiage, but because the neighbors don't mind, it's not an issue. Conversely, we once parked in front of my parent's house while my dad helped install the front door he'd custom built, and their neighbors called us in as an eyesore!

How do you transform the driver's seat into your "office"?

Our front window panels are one of my favorite strokes of

genius we had while building. They're incredibly simple – just Reflectix covered over with thin, painted wood paneling. The effect is that of "walls" over the windows, but in reality, they slip easily in and out. Besides the aesthetic, they help retain heat in the winter and keep the sun out in summer to keep the front cooler.

What was the total cost of the bus?

We purchased the bus for five thousand and spent another twenty renovating it. Since then, we've done multiple upgrades that have added maybe a thousand or so to that total.

How long did it take to convert the bus?

A year total, but as you'll recall, it sat half-finished for about six months of that time. We purchased it in May and moved in almost a year to the day later.

Do you have to put everything on your shelves away when you move?

Nope! We use a mix of museum wax, command strips, and elastic bungee cords over the fronts of our shelves to keep everything in places while we drive. In one of my sneakiest tricks, I used clear plastic bra straps and home décor screws to create nearly invisible straps across our books. In a video that went viral on TikTok, I received so many comments concerned about all the books that would go flying into the back of my head if I braked too hard, I actually had to post a follow-up showing off the magic of the recycled bra straps! Almost everything you see in the bus when it's parked stays that way when we drive. The exception is the dash area; the plants ride in the shower and the art is removed so I can safely drive with my field of view unimpaired.

How do you do laundry?

For the first bit of time while we had a combo washer and dryer, we used it. But having to be plugged in because of its power requirements was a real bummer, so we removed it and now utilize laundry facilities at laundry mats and friend's and family's homes. In a pinch, we can also use our wood wine barrel bathtub to hand wash, and then dry it on the clothesline we carry with us attached to the bus.

How does the drain in your bathroom work?

Beneath the wood slatted tiles, we have a regular bathtub drain that works just like the one in a stick-built home. Because we don't use chemicals or store-bought home and body care items, preferring ones we've made from natural ingredients, we normally allow the water to free drain. If the situation calls for it, we have a portable gray tank we can position under the main drain to catch water. The bathtub isn't plumbed in, which allows me to use it outdoors as well as in, and it simply drains into the shower through the hole in the bottom.

Do you have space under the bus and what do you keep there?

We do! Four doors lead to one very large space that's roughly a third the length of our bus. For the first two years, it held our water tanks, solar equipment, camping gear, wood for our stove, and tools. As I write this, however, we're preparing to move our water tanks and solar equipment under the bed, leaving more space in the underbelly for storage.

How do you get mail?

When we're traveling, we have it sent along our destination to friends and family or Amazon pick-up locations if it's important. If it's not imperative we receive it right away, we simply have it sent to home base.

How did you find your bus?

A client at our gym had a husband who happened to be a diesel mechanic at a local trucking company. They also sold school buses, and Oliver came in on a routine trade deal with a local high school when they purchased new buses. Having a friend who knew so much about buses helped, because he was able to guide us to exactly the right one while steering us away from those that would be expensive to work on down the line or have bigger issues.

What are the downsides?

Well there's a whole chapter on that! But in a few words, temperature regulation, filling tanks, having a home with an engine that requires regular maintenance, and not being able to take a long, hot shower whenever you feel like it. Then there are necessary evils like laundry mats, Wi-Fi chasing, and parking concerns. Oh, and if you're not a huge fan of Wal-Mart parking lots, bus life might not be for you either.

Is the bus insured?

Yes. We have a full RV policy, along with renter's insurance for items we leave at Evan's now, like Mike's blacksmithing forge and related equipment.

What if someone tries to rob you or take the bus?

There's a part of me that always wants to answer this one flippantly. Like, have you seen the man I live with? But in all seriousness, it's not something I worry about, not any more than I would have in our old home. As a matter of fact, I was home alone at night when someone *did* try to break into our old home. The alarm went off on a downstairs window as someone tried to crawl through it, and I stood at the top of the steps with my gun until the cops arrived. Thankfully, whoever had thought it might be a good idea quickly changed their mind and left and that was the end of it. I've never had anything even remotely that scary happen in the bus. Worst case scenario, I suppose, is they succeed, and in that event I simply wish them luck trying to hide the large white branded school bus that is my home from authorities for very long with all the cameras on roadways nowadays, and ask they please make sure to fill the tanks with the right fuel. Oliver is rather picky.

What do you do about heating and cooling?

We have a Jotul wood stove that keeps us warm in the winter, and a diesel heater as a backup. We're all about redundancy in bus life when it comes to being prepared. We use a window unit for air conditioning while we're parked and plugged in, and screens for our windows and doors when we can't plug in. When we travel, we tend to chase mild weather that doesn't require extreme measures to stay comfortable.

What if something happens to one of you while you're out in the wild?

I carry a fairly extensive medical bag with us on the bus, a
remnant from the nursing school days and my time working in
the field. Between us, we have enough training and supplies to
deal with most emergencies, at least long enough to temporarily
manage while we drove back into civilization or waited for
responders to come. Mike and I may be somewhat impulsive in
our decision making, but we're thorough planners as we move
along our chosen path and believers in redundancy. Being able
to stay safely off-grid was a huge part of our planning process,
both physically and functionally, and should top your priority
list if you're considering a similar life.

Is it hard to find places to park a bus that size?

It really depends on where we are. In cities, absolutely yes, it's
harder. We stick mainly to large store lots, where RVs are
generally allowed to take up several spots in the back of it
without issue. Outside of cities, it's much easier than you might
think. Most large tourist attractions, like national parks and
points of interest along major highways, have RV parking spots

available. On public lands, which is mostly what we stick to, it's even easier, just a simple matter of scouting out the possibilities and choosing the best one. At the end of the day, you make what you have work. After a particularly long driving day, we once parked facing downhill on the side of a mountain next to an electrical station on what was barely a road, because night was falling and the next marked stop was sixty miles away. The wind shook the bus all night as it howled around us, and in the morning we were literally walking downhill toward our kitchen to make coffee, but it did the job and we were on our way shortly after, where we would find the most glorious and remote spot we'd ever encountered, one we certainly would have missed in the dark the night before, a mere half hour away.

Is driving hard?

There is a definite learning curve. After three years driving him around, I'm fairly confident, but it wasn't always that way. There were lots of places I wouldn't go in that first year as I adjusted to driving a forty-foot tube. The main considerations are reversing and turning. Right hand turns, especially, require some practice to execute smoothly, without hopping onto a curb or pulling out too far into traffic. Finding the specific pivot point of your bus (ours is just before the rear tire) and watching for it to clear the corner before turning hard is the main piece of advice I can give there. For reversing, we now have three cameras that help immensely. By watching my monitor, I can see exactly how close I am on my sides and rear to help me park more easily. Before that, I either had to wing it or have someone outside directing me into tight spots.

Would you do it all again?

Yes.

About the Author

Tawny McVay is the creator behind the popular social media channels and website this book is inspired by, where she shares daily life in the school bus she converted into a tiny home with her husband, Mike. Before uprooting their lives, the pair lived and breathed fitness, training at the gym they started in Montana. While it was hard to say goodbye to their community of members, Tawny has discovered there's a lot of life to be lived outside the weight room. Her greatest joys are creating beautiful meals in her tiny kitchen, a gorgeous sunset to enjoy over a cup of coffee, and the feel of a plane ticket in her hand.

See more at: **www.sincewewokeup.com**
Social media: **@sincewewokeup**
Inquiries: **info@sincewewokeup.com**

Made in United States
North Haven, CT
21 December 2024

63102144R10153